WAITING FOR THE LORD

Meditation Themes

by

REV. MSGR. WILLIAM L. DOTY

Author of:

"The On-Going Pilgrimage"

"Prayer in the Spirit"

"Encountering Christian Crises"

WAITING FOR THE LORD

Meditation Themes

by William L. Doty

ALBA · HOUSE   NEW · YORK

SOCIETY OF ST. PAUL, 2187 VICTORY BLVD., STATEN ISLAND, NEW YORK 10314

Library of Congress Cataloging in Publication Data

Doty, William Lodewick, 1919-
  Waiting for the Lord.

  1. Meditations. I. Title.
BX2182.2.D64   242   76-45384
ISBN 0-8189-0338-4

Nihil Obstat:
Daniel V. Flynn, J.C.D.
Censor Librorum

Imprimatur:
✝ *James P. Mahoney, D.D.*
Vicar General, Archdiocese of New York
September 16, 1976

Designed, printed and bound in the United States of
America by the Fathers and Brothers of the Society of St. Paul,
2187 Victory Boulevard, Staten Island, New York, 10314,
as part of their communications apostolate.

1 2 3 4 5 6 7 8 9 (Current Printing: first digit).

DEDICATION:

To the Rev. Msgr. William J. Walsh

"I was sick and you came to me."

AUTHOR'S NOTE

The following short chapters are not so much meditations as points of departure for meditation. Although they are not arranged in any special order, a reading of them all will, it is hoped, supply a sufficient number of relevant themes to assist the reader in reflecting fruitfully on many aspects of the Christian life which need emphasis in our time. The book is directed to priests, religious, and lay persons dedicated to "prayer in the Spirit."

CONTENTS

Meditation Themes

1.

WAITING

The thirtieth chapter of Isaiah contains verses which are now used in the liturgy of the church at compline. Verses 15 and 18 are put together to form the following (if the Douay version is used):

"If you return and be quiet, you shall be saved: in silence and in hope shall your strength be . . . Therefore the Lord waiteth that He may have mercy on you . . . Because the Lord is the God of judgment; blessed are all they that wait for Him."

In the turmoil and high-pressure atmosphere of our times, the words in this quotation take on a special meaning; words such as "quiet", "silence", "hope", "strength", and especially, perhaps, the word "wait". Significantly we are told that the Lord waits to have mercy on us and then in turn we are instructed that "blessed are all they that wait for Him."

It might be advantageous from time to time, particularly in the midst of the pressures and anxieties of a busy life, to meditate on this section of the Bible, to try to apply it to one's life by seeing its implications in terms of the later revelations and example of Christ.

The thrust of these verses is not particularly popular today. Quiet, perseverance in waiting, these are not things that are rated high on the scale of modern values. Aggressiveness, relying on one's self as the total source of one's strength, and seeking to attain

objectives in the shortest and most efficient manner, are impera-
tives in our times. Modern man is not known for his willingness to
play a waiting role; one must be up and doing, must be a go-get-
ter, must bring home the bacon, win the race, come out on top,
"make it big." If failure is the greatest evil, then having to wait
patiently for a long time is the second greatest disaster. The fact
that everyone cannot be a chief and that there must be some rank
and file Indians, plus the additional fact that every objective cannot be attained expeditiously despite enormous advances in technology, does not dissipate the thrust toward immediate attainment.
Unfortunately mass frustration and neurosis are the frequent
result of the inability to wait in quiet trust.

Everyone has known persons who have been unwilling to
persevere trustingly. There is the young fellow who drops out of
school and directs his steps on the path of a wasteful life because
he has failed three subjects and cannot persevere on the way to
self-improvement. There is the young married couple who, run-
ning into misunderstandings and conflicts in the early stages of
their marriage, prefer to break up rather than to try to work it out
on a long term basis. There is the brilliant lawyer who, convicted
of fraud, takes his own life rather than strive to reshape his life
after prison. There is the young executive who, denied a promotion, seeks refuge in drink rather than in renewed determination
to persevere in his vocation. There is the widow who, losing her
beloved husband through death, confronts her loss bitterly and
turns away from the practice of her faith. And then there is the
more common case of the individual who finds no satisfactory
response to his prayers of petition and hence gives up prayer
and confidence in God's responsiveness almost entirely.

These people have forgotten or perhaps have been entirely
ignorant of the clear messages in both the Old and the New
Testaments about the importance of quiet, persevering, waiting
upon God's mercy. Not only Isaiah but Jesus stresses the importance of this confident waiting attitude. "Blessed is he whom the
master shall find waiting," He tells us in His parable of the absent
master and the faithful servant. Because the master seems a long

time coming, He tells us, is no reason for the servant to lose confidence in the master and turn away from his rule concerning the governance of life. Jesus, again, indicates that an important element of prayer is trustful perseverance when He gives us the little parable of the man who won't get out of bed to give his neighbor three loaves during the night. He says that if the neighbor continues knocking, eventually the master of the house will get up and give him what he wants if only to get rid of him. By such homely examples He made it clear that one knock on God's door may not be enough. We must keep knocking and keep waiting. "Therefore the Lord waiteth that He may have mercy on you." "Blessed are all they that wait for Him."

There is a twofold waiting then: God waits and man waits. This mystery of mutual waiting is worthy of serious reflection. In some ways it goes to the very root of human history and even of human existence. The whole process of history, after all, is one of expectation, of waiting for the ultimate fulfillment: "Thy kingdom come." Revelation, the final book of the New Testament, utters this heart's cry of mankind for fulfillment: "Come, Lord Jesus, come."

But God waits on us as well. "Therefore the Lord waiteth that He may have mercy on you." He waits for our conversion, for our perfection, made possible to us through His Spirit. Normally He does not take us in our sins; in His mercy He permits us to follow the long path, the long pilgrimage, through its by-ways, its hills and valleys, its periods of lost direction, sometimes its sense of never-endingness. He knows that through all this our attitudes may be purified, our need for trust made evident, our awareness of dependency upon Him nourished. "In silence and in hope shall your strength be." It is on the long, long trail, often with no immediate goal in view, that we find the power of quiet perseverance. And as He said to St. Paul, "Power is made perfect in infirmity." But He accompanied that by the words: "My grace is sufficient for thee."

If, among contemporary Catholics, Teilhard de Chardin has shown us something of the Creator's purpose in setting in motion a long process of evolution to the human level, a process that seems staggering in terms of the long wait of millions of years, modern man should not be entirely surprised at the evolutionary design of his own individual life, especially in terms of his development as a spiritually mature person. There is a waiting process here on all sides. Nevertheless it is precisely a process and therefore not static. It is a moving forward and yet a waiting; a waiting and yet a source of strength. "In silence and in hope shall your strength be." One accepts whatever light and strength one receives to move along the path to God and yet one waits for fresh outpourings, for new openings, for more profound mercies. "Because the Lord is the God of judgment (justice); blessed are all they that wait for Him."

It seems to be true that everyone has his "hour" which comes in God's good time. Jesus Himself said at Cana, "My hour has not yet come." But the hour came indeed on Calvary, an hour which opened up to the Resurrection and the endless hour of eternal life.

The wait is sometimes long but we must not grow weary; we must not lose our quiet hope. God has spoken through Isaiah (and later more fulfillingly in Christ): "If you return and be quiet, you shall be saved."

2.

WORD POWER

In the first chapter of his Epistle to the Philippians, St. Paul speaks enthusiastically of the fact that "Most of my brothers in Christ, taking courage from my chains, have been further emboldened to speak the word of God fearlessly." Then he goes on to note that "It is true, some preach Christ from motives of envy and rivalry, but others do so out of good will." One would think that Paul would find this envious preaching worthless. On the contrary he states: "What of it? All that matters is that in any and every way, whether from specious motives or genuine ones, Christ is being proclaimed! That is what brings me joy."

These comments of St. Paul are interesting because they not only stress the importance of proclaiming the word of God but also indicate that this word has a sort of power of itself even apart from the motivations of those who proclaim it. By what is clearly a too narrow view of the matter, many Christians, contemporary and otherwise, have fallen into the habit of thinking that the efficacy of the word of God is entirely dependent upon the virtuousness of the preacher. This attitude resembles in a way the Montanist heresy of the early centuries, which tended to regard the administration of the sacraments as ineffective unless the minister himself possessed the state of grace. As in the case of grace in the sacraments, the truth of God remains truth however sullied the lips from which it emerges. However base the motivation, the light of the words can shine through and touch the hearts of the listeners. This divine word power is in a sense intrinsic in the word itself; its effectiveness is revealed primarily in conjunction with God-given graces which it occasions in the hearts of those who receive it.

That the proclaiming of the word might be substantially more effective if the motivations and the spirituality of the proclaimers were of a high level was not contested by Paul or by any other ecclesiastical source. The only point stressed is that the power of God's revealed word is not totally dependent on factors outside itself. The fact of primary importance is that "Christ is being proclaimed."

Far from encouraging poor motivation or indifference, this emphasis of St. Paul can help strengthen the timid and reluctant to speak out more valiantly, despite the recognition of their own limitations both in piety and communication. Observation would lead one to believe that many Christians, and perhaps most Catholics, are extremely reluctant to utter the "saving word" even when circumstances are propitious. Preaching, they feel, is something better left to the clergy and the pulpit.

Even apart from the fact that laymen feel ill-equipped to proclaim the word, they tend to have an aversion to preachments of any type in the ordinary course of daily life. This is no doubt the result of priggish and pietistical proclamations by self-righteous individuals whose concept of the Christian gospel is largely that of condemnatory ethic. But suitable reflection upon the matter readily reveals that the saving word is neither primarily condemnatory nor merely ethical, but rather strengthening, healing, redeeming, joyfully transforming. The saving word is the Christian word of consolation to the depressed, the downtrodden, the deprived, the bereft. It is the word of Christ applied to moments of fear, of anxiety, of loneliness as well as moments of hope and love and fruition.

One basic requirement is that it be precisely the word of the gospel and not merely psychological or secular counsel. These latter may have considerable merit but this value can never equal that of the proclaimed words of Christ. And yet it must be a matter of amazement to non-Christians that those who claim to be sincere followers of Christ utter His words so infrequently even in the deepest moments of crisis, unless it be to use His Name blasphemously.

These considerations suggest that Christians should not only be well-read in the Scriptures but that they should commit to memory key phrases and passages which are applicable to the various circumstances of human living. Self-consciousness and obviousness can be swept aside in the intrinsic power of the text. The manner of presentation may vary but the importance is that "Christ is being proclaimed." This is a blessing both to the hearer and the proclaimer. One does not have to pass out printed texts, although this is not to be sneered at. But to carry a New Testament and to read from it when the situation warrants need not be nearly as difficult as assumed. Why could not one Christian say to another in need: "I think I remember a passage from the gospel which might be helpful to you in this situation. May I share it with you?" Then the proclaimer could simply read the text. What hurting person could fail to be moved by such an offer? He can only come to appreciate more deeply the power of the gospel word to heal and to save.

The second Vatican Council, so modern in its thinking, emphasized the importance of such proclamation of the word of God. It stressed the power of Christian example but, no more than St. Paul, or than Christ Himself, was it satisfied with example alone. It is the word that gives meaning to the example, a fuller dimension, a larger scope and influence and insight. The sacraments have never consisted of actions alone; the meaningful form has always consisted of words. There are many atheists who perform generous actions but these in themselves can offer little if any testimony to Christ, unless by reminding Christians of their own deficiency.

The importance of proclaiming the word to others should not lead us to minimize the equal importance of proclaiming it to ourselves. We can and should be both preacher and listener at the same time. The power in God's word is just as much present to the one who utters as to the one who listens. The fact that both utterer and hearer are the same does not weaken the effect. The spiritual writers have often emphasized the importance of brief aspirations, short prayers to God uttered in a second or two when devotion or need suggests. The same suggestion is valid with respect to the word of God. In fact, the utterance of a scriptural word has the power of Christ's Spirit within it. It is not only a plea for grace; it is a medium of grace. Christ comes in His word in a sort of communion, the strengthening power of which can be experienced at once. To have in one's mind and one's heart, readily available, appropriate verses of Holy Scripture, is to have Christ present in every need and situation, with His guidance, His consolation, His benediction.

St. Paul said that the important thing is that "Christ is being proclaimed." The modern Christian should meditate on his own reluctance to do what is so important. It is so important because the Christian life cannot exist without the *word* of life.

3.

THE THIRD WAY

When we examine the example of St. Thomas More, who is in many ways the model of the Christian humanist, we are led to ask ourselves if there is "a third way" of Christian conduct opposed both to weak compromise and to adamant rigidity. More did everything possible to serve both God and king. It was only at the very end, when he recognized that it was impossible to satisfy the king without rejecting God and His church, that he stood upon the scaffold and uttered the famous words: "I die the king's good servant, but God's first."

Notice that, without ever considering for a moment that he would offend God for the sake of the king, he nevertheless explored every possibility whereby he might harmonize his political conduct with his allegiance to Christ. He did not immediately adopt an attitude of rigidity because, in his deep humanism, he realized that frequently neither God nor man is best served by failing to explore alternative possibilities of action in what seems to be a moral crisis.

Modern Christians would do well to reflect upon some of the principles of this third way, this way of Christian humanism.

(1) The Christian humanist, in the spirit of Christ, who said "I am come that they may have life and have it more abundantly," seeks to preserve and enhance all possible human values in a given situation. His first consideration therefore is positive, unifying, peace making. He abhors confrontations which involve the suppression or destruction of one value in favor of another. He would

prefer if possible to harmonize interests so that all may emerge in the situation more richly. He senses that in human life there are relatively few situations in which one side is totally right and the other totally wrong. He wishes to draw out and to support whatever genuine good may be present on either or many sides. His normal tendency is to take the largest possible view of human problems, conflicts, and dilemmas, trying to place them in the most transcendental and far-seeing perspective so that all elements may be properly illuminated and evaluated. Because he is on the side of life, he will meditate long and hard before he chooses a course of action which may be damaging or death-dealing to any authentic human value.

(2) Although he will try to give full weight to all factors, the Christian humanist recognizes that at times he must insist upon certain priorities. He knows and will not deny that obedience to God comes before obedience to men, that one may not help a neighbor by being unjust to someone else, and that the preservation of truth is more important than immediate advantages to be gained by substantial lies. But, despite his recognition of priorities, he will not readily admit that extremes in opposition of one virtue to another are frequently necessary human conditions. Nor will he deny that various circumstances may be frequently altered in such a way as to accommodate all factors in reasonable degree.

Thus he may often be willing to sacrifice his own interests as long as these interests are not required by unshakable moral principles. For example, rather than engage in a disruptive argument in which charity may well be seriously damaged, he will sacrifice his right to reply, his right of self-defense, or his right to certain other advantages. In so doing he will have in mind the larger values of peace and harmony through which suitable remedies may eventually emerge.

(3) On the other hand, he will not be too quick to rule out immediately a course of action which may seem on the surface to be unwarrantable. He will first reflect on the laws of God and man, the dictates of the gospel, the guidelines of the church's magisterium, and the special circumstances of this particular case,

and only then will he do his best to extract the solution which is appropriate, in accordance with the essential humanism of the Christian gospel.

Although he will recognize the inflexibility of certain principles of morality, which cannot be changed by mere difficult and painful circumstances, he will also be highly conscious of the fact that in some cases circumstances *do* alter cases. He will weigh the circumstances carefully to see if a higher principle may not sometimes be invoked to open a way out of what seemed to be a dilemma between harshly opposing extremes. He will be keenly aware that most positive laws, whether of society or of the church, are not intended to bind under grave inconvenience, although the same cannot always be said of negative or forbidding laws. Although he will confirm the value of reasonable positive laws and will do his best to preserve their values, he will not allow his conscience to be tainted by a scrupulous legalism, which in the long run becomes an enemy of humanity and undermines the very laws which it purports to preserve.

(4) The Christian humanist will have a special disposition to preserve and enhance human freedom, especially the freedom to move towards one's end as a son of God, participating in divine life. Since he knows that this freedom is attained and fulfilled by carrying out the will of the Father in Heaven, he recognizes it as a sublimely responsible freedom. He looks to the life of Christ, Who said, "I do always the things that please Him," as a pathway to a liberation that begins here and finds its completion in eternity.

But because the concern of God as manifested in Christ is for the enhancement of all human beings in the attainment of their end, the Christian humanist as a loyal son of God cannot remain indifferent when unjust restrictions are placed on his brothers. Although obviously prudence and his own limitations in knowledge and sensitivity will cause him to be reasonably reserved in criticizing or attempting to bring about the repeal of disturbing laws, he will, when necessary, do all that he can in accordance with the principles of the Christian gospel to bring about the correction of those laws which are obviously opposed to the common good or to the basic rights of individuals. He will feel that arbitrary commands from on high, without due consultation with those who are to enforce the law or even with those who are to be subject to it, have a certain inhuman quality in that they may well show a special contempt for the intelligence and dignity of mankind. In this context his devotion to God-given liberty will find expression in the dictum: "The minimum of law and the maximum of freedom inasmuch as the promotion of the common and individual good allows."

(5) The Christian humanist in his devotion to the "third way," although he will come down strongly on the side of individual liberty, will never limit his attention to the merely individual good but will have in mind the consequences of his decisions upon the common weal of the larger group, whether it be the church, or society, or some other community of which he is a part. He will often sacrifice his just rights for the sake of some larger good. He will, moreover, encourage others to do the same. But his encouragement of this type of sacrificial action will always be accompanied by stress on the personal individual growth which becomes possible thereby. For him it is not a question of frustrating oneself, draining oneself of possibilities, negating one's own human nature for some remote or abstract common good. It is a question of genuine human sacrifice in behalf of others, a sacrifice which because it takes place in the context of a higher love, of a reaching out for God in himself and in other human beings, is in the long run not demeaning but enhancing to self as well as to others. The Christian humanist knows that the spiritual joy and reward of generous sacrifice far transcend what some non-Christian humanists regard as personal self-fulfillment. The Christian humanist knows that the soul expands when it loves, that sacrifice for others is not only the test but the fruit of a liberated love.

But, despite his devotion to the apparent good of other humans, there are lines that he will not cross, laws that he will not evade. He will do everything possible to serve the king and serve the humblest subject of the king. But he will end with the words of More: "I die the king's good servant, but God's first."

4.

SUPPORTIVENESS

One of the most striking examples of supportiveness in the New Testament occurs during the passion of Christ when Simon the Cyrenean helps Christ to carry His cross. The gospel tells us that Simon was made to do this by the Roman soldiers, but we may assume that his spirit of compassion was such that, even if he were reluctant in the beginning, he came more and more to realize the blessedness of his opportunity. The Christian tradition has always venerated him as one who supported Jesus in the hour of His greatest crisis.

Certain conclusions result from meditation on this scene:

(1) Simon's helpfulness did not remove the burden of Christ completely but rather made it more tolerable, presumably, than it had been before. Simon added just enough support to enable Christ to reach the place of His death, which was also the place of His victory. Even though Jesus had divine powers available to Him, we must conclude that, humanly speaking, He was so physically weak as to be unable to continue the bloody pilgrimage unaided. His Father did not will that Jesus use miraculous powers in this situation; rather it was the providential plan that Christ should be supported in His task by a human person, using purely human powers.

This scene emphasizes the fact that the support of others is necessary to all of us on the sometimes bloody pilgrimage to our own goal of "life through death." This is too obvious for comment on the purely physical and even on the intellectual level but men all too frequently may forget to support Christ in others when others are stumbling along with over-heavy crosses of grief or temptation or desolation. There is a tendency to be like the other spectators on the Calvary route: to look on with a certain complacency at the sufferings of others and not even to think of putting one's shoulder under the cross.

But, as the Gospel scene suggests, often only a very little help is needed and is sufficient. Commentators have never thought that Simon's burden was really very heavy. He probably supplied just that little supportiveness that made all the difference between collapse and perseverance in an upright posture. In most human situations a little bit of help is all that is needed in overcoming obstacles and attaining desired goals. Indeed the very fact that another person is concerned, even though he offers very little practical help, can tip the scales in favor of survival and accomplishment.

A priest who was newly appointed as a chaplain at a home for incurable cancer patients was told on the day of his arrival the following: "Father," the sister in charge said, "this may seem like an enormous task to you, strengthening these people spiritually to live out the last days or months of their lives in a spirit of Christian joy and hope. No doubt it seems almost an impossibility. And so I just want to tell you, Father, all that these people ask is a little kindness, a little concern. You don't have to undertake any grave or arduous task; simply say a few spiritually encouraging words to them each day to show that Christ and His church are concerned about them and they will respond in a manner which seems beyond belief. Just give them a little support, Father, and under God they will do the rest."

The subsequent experience of the priest confirmed her words. By his regular administration of the sacraments and his simple words of encouragement the impossible was accomplished: they were enabled to carry their crosses profitably to the end.

(2) Tradition maintains that Simon of Cyrene was converted

to an ardent Christian by reason of his act of supportiveness. We may well believe it. The Gospel and our whole Christian experience make clear that God is never outdone in generosity. We need only to make a small gesture of helpfulness, to take one step forward, to carry one small part of the burden of Christ, and a new strength is bestowed upon us, new possibilities for enhancement are opened out to us. It is the basic Christian paradox: in helping others we are helping ourselves; in denying the self we find new life; in giving a mite we receive a hundredfold. Even on the purely natural level we are told by psychologists that to go out of ourselves in order to assist others, however slightly, will often relieve our own depression and give us a fresh taste of the joy of living. In terms of grace and the Christian life the rewards are proportionately and indeed qualitatively greater. St. Matthew's Gospel speaks of eternal life as the bounty bestowed upon those who assist Christ in others: "Whatever you do to the least of these, my brethren, you do unto Me." And the supportiveness which we are called upon to give others is really not that difficult: a cup of cold water, a visit to the sick, a word of comfort to those confined, and the like. But the effect on both the giver and the receiver is far greater than the mere action or object itself. There is a communication of God and God's strength in the act of supportiveness—a mutual communication whereby both parties are enhanced.

(3) In meditating upon Simon carrying the cross we must remember that in the beginning he was probably not yet a follower of the Lord. In looking around us in the contemporary world we are perhaps a little ashamed to see how ready non-Christians or even nominal Christians are to lend supportiveness to worthy causes and to needy individuals. We think of psychiatrists and psychologists, who certainly could have chosen some easier way to make a living, spending hours and hours each day listening to the troubles of others and offering them the supportive interest and purposefulness which can bring them through their trials. This is sometimes known as paid friendship, it is true, but on the whole the efforts of these professional persons undoubtedly go

far beyond the mere minimum of mechanical presence and rote counselling. They are concerned human beings helping others in trouble and it is their genuine concern which will be curative in proportion to its humaneness. Supportive therapy is the key factor in the amelioration of most neuroses and mental illnesses. Even apart from professionals in the field, most troubled individuals find that warm-hearted and generous concern on the part of even one friend or acquaintance can help them through difficulties which would appear otherwise impassable. Very often these friends or acquaintances, just like the psychiatrist and psychologist, are not notable for their Christian commitment.

This is an occasion for self-examination, a reassessment on the part of those who consider themselves authentic Christians. We are reminded of the parable of the Good Samaritan, who was outside the pale of Jewish orthodoxy, and yet put the priest and Levite to shame. Sometimes even the most dedicated Christians become so concerned with liturgicalism, new trends in theology, new Christian movements and new methods of prayer or social action that they neglect the ready opportunities which abound on every side to say a supportive word, to lend an assisting hand or even a willing ear to those individuals who are struggling along Calvary road and need just the slightest support to bear up; yet without that slight support they will certainly fall.

Christians sometimes feel that only great sacrifices are worthy of their participation. The Cyreneans of our time know better: putting one's shoulder beneath another's cross is not a great sacrifice in itself but it can result in one's being caught up in the great and transforming and life-giving sacrifice of the "Man for Others."

5.

NON-INTIMIDATION

Have you ever noticed how Gospel texts that you have read often without any noticeable reaction, suddenly, on the thousand and first reading, seem to speak to you keenly and profoundly? They take on a whole new dimension and relevancy and seem to answer some deep question or problem that is challenging you at the moment. That of course may be the reason they never impressed you particularly in the past: thet fact that you never had any real need for them in your own life. But now in a new context, a new confluence of circumstances, God seems to be speaking to you through the sacred word—a direct sort of message meant in a special way for the existential moment. It is, no doubt, in a certain sense a revelation, at least of a private sort.

A priest recently said the following: "I had such a revelation experience recently when I was reading the Sunday Gospel and proclaimed the words of Christ: 'Do not be intimidated by men.' This of course was not advice to nervous ladies, but to His own disciples, urging them, as it were, to put aside human fears of what other people might think or do; to take assurance that He would strengthen and provide for them in the proclamation of His word.

"This touched me because I had been feeling certain vague fears in connection with my ministry as pastor of this parish. Some of the people here—a small minority, it is true—are very touchy and make all sorts of protests and trouble if you happen to annoy them either by words from the altar or by changes in the traditional routine or by some other pastoral decision which infringes on their preferred way of doing. When you have had two or three experiences with such vociferous and strong-minded people you become timid about any strong statements or innovative procedures. There is a temptation to be bland and oily and never to allow yourself to pronounce an absolute negative or even too strong an affirmative. If you give in to the repressive atmosphere created by such persons you are led to straddle the pastoral fence and prefer a peaceful mediocrity to a probably tempestuous launching out into the deep.

"Then one does not want to offend the liberal element either for they have their own ways of retribution, such as abstaining from Mass attendance, marrying outside the Church, or refusing to send their children to religious instruction. To avoid trouble one is inclined to be mild in one's attack upon the sexual mores of the times. One does not want to drive the young people out the door of the church even though many of them are already standing in the vestibule. Hell and damnation are, of course, not even indirectly to be alluded to.

"To tell the people from the next parish to go to their own church because they are crowding your Sunday masses beyond endurance would be a *faux pas* of the worst type. To scold that large segment of the congregation which has not increased its Sunday offering in the last twenty years might well mean even less in the following week's collection. The words of Jesus about not being intimidated struck me in my nervous state as a necessary, helpful antibiotic."

But there are other fears known not only to pastors but to every Christian. Such things as the hesitancy to speak of religious matters in the presence of the irreligious, the reluctance to try to influence a lapsed Catholic, even in one's own family, to attend church, the fear of getting too involved in church organizations and activities, the timidity about seeking spiritual counsel or even absolution—these are a few of the barriers which we find it hard to surmount simply because we are intimidated by men. Perhaps the most devastating fear is that of responding too generously to the movements of the Holy Spirit lest we be trapped into living out the full Christian life in all its implications of sacrifice and self-denial. But this, of course, is not being intimidated by men but in a sense by ourselves, by our own weakness, our own selfishness.

"Do not be intimidated by men." Do these words have a still wider application or are they limited merely to the acting out of the ministry? Since a Christian is always a Christian and since everything he does is or should be related to the glory of God and the salvation of souls in Christ, however indirectly, the strengthening admonition by Christ could be applied to the whole spectrum of our attitudes and actions. Even anxiety-neurotics could benefit greatly from meditating on these words, but certainly timid Christians could take heart from them. Who among us does not have at times vague anxieties related to day-by-day relationships with others? Many fear to meet new people, to enter into new situations, to expose themselves in one way or another to the critical view of others. Many of us view the day's scene with a certain nervous horror, particularly at the first waking moments of the day. At times one just does not feel equipped to carry on; to wrap oneself in the cocoon of separation from all the day's trials seems highly desirable. The thought of escape is dominant. Dependents may even be uncounseled and important work left undone. The words of Christ have found no resonance: "Do not be intimidated by men."

But how can these words become effective? There are many answers, no doubt, but the pastor's comments are interesting:

"When timidity and fears begin to unsettle me I simply sit down in my chair and spend a few minutes meditating on the words of Christ about not being intimidated. I think too of other texts such as 'Fear not, it is I,' or 'Why are you fearful, O you of little faith?' or 'The hairs of your head are all numbered,' or the saying about the Father's care for the sparrows and how much more precious I am in the Father's eyes than many sparrows. I think too of some of Paul's sayings, especially 'I can do all things in Him Who strengthens me.' I try to open my soul and mind and heart to the inflowing power of God. I ask Him to permeate me—my mind, my will, my heart, my very being with His strength. I make bold to remind God that I am His instrument and that the work that I am doing is His work. The Old Testament locution will often be in my mind, 'Unless the Lord build the house, they labor in vain who build it,'

"In such a context it inevitably comes over me that what I am afraid of is some sort of damage to my own ego, to my own inflated self-image. I am afraid of effort because it will damage my self-indulgence, but especially of failure by exposure of my weakness to others, because this will plunge a spear into the very heart of my pride. My timidity then is normally not founded in reasonable anxiety but in an over-anxiousness to protect myself from pain of one type or another. My concern is not really for God or His work or His purposes in me or in others but for my inflated self.

"Therefore, when I view what challenges confront me as a follower of Christ I can, through meditation, remove them from the altar of the ego and place them in God's hands as challenges to be met by His strength in me. In the words of St. John the Baptist, 'He must increase, while I must decrease.' I tell myself that with Christ working within me for His purposes and not mine I can have no fear. The success or failure of my mission is His to decide, His to accomplish. My strength is not mine but His. My accomplishment is not mine but His. My rejection, if it occurs, is not mine but His.

Do not be intimidated by men. A few minutes' meditation along these lines can accomplish wonders in dissipating idle fears. When at last I can say with St. Paul, "I live now, not I, but Christ lives in me," the last trace of timidity will be banished.

6.

WITNESS OR MANIPULATION?

Those who seek to do apostolic work for Christ learn one thing early on: people are not to be manipulated. You can bear witness to people, you can teach them, you can even persuade them, but there is something inherent in humans which resists the dehumanizing attempt to manipulate them as though they were objects instead of responsible free agents.

No doubt everyone at some time or another has had the experience of trying to bend another person to his will without making sufficient allowance for the other's personal dignity. Parents find this a constant problem in trying to guide and direct their own children. Even a small child, not merely out of stubbornness but out of a sense of his own dignity, will resist the arbitrariness and forcefulness of a parent's effort to make him conform. The more inhuman the pressure becomes the more stubborn the child's resistance. On the other hand, the child knows that he must respect the freedom of his parents to choose whether or not they will comply with his wishes. How often the child has heard his parents say, "I won't give it to you unless you say 'please'."

As life goes on, we all find that our home experiences are re-enacted in all sorts of human relationships. The overbearing, down-putting superior gets little work from his subordinates and the over-aggressive worker who keeps pressing his boss unduly for more power and money is likely to defeat his own purposes.

Manipulation, however, is not confined to those who adopt an overbearing attitude toward others. We all know that the flatterer, the deceiver, the person who appeals to lust or other baser instincts may be equally as guilty and even more successful in his manipulating efforts.

Without fear of making an overly sweeping condemnation of modern advertising, even the most unprejudiced observer can detect many of these elements in certain ad programs. There can be little doubt that the advertising agency figures out in advance precisely those most vulnerable areas of motivation and then proceeds to direct all possible verbal and pictorial artillery against them. The displays, the nudity, the blatant stroking of the human tendency to self-indulgence, the ill-concealed appeal to snobbery, are only some of the elements that are carefully packaged to lead the public to buy something useless or relatively useless. Such advertising is a cynical method of manipulation because it appeals not to individuals as genuine human persons but as mere biological mechanisms which can be made to respond by appropriate pressures.

Justly or unjustly, politicians are often thought to be the most flagrant manipulators of their fellow men. It is almost a cliché of the political world that the highly intelligent man who discusses political problems in a clear and well-balanced fashion and offers carefully reasoned solutions is very unlikely to win elections on those grounds alone. No, it is necessary for expert public relations people to package him like a commodity, to hype up his program so that it has something in it to appeal to the prejudices of the most numerous minorities. Moreover, he must look the part of a strong sympathetic man of the people who is not afraid to roll up his shirtsleeves and mix with the sweating crowd, eating hot dogs all the while. He must have his hair curled and his eyebrows tweezed, and his suit made on Savile Row, while the intellectual integrity of his program is played down in favor of whatever mob appeal he can conjure up.

All necessary elements are evaluated and scored upon charts. If his present image is ineffective, a new image must be created before it is too late. Truth, integrity, higher values, respect for the intelligence and dignity of others, even of those who may not be in full control of their passions and prejudices, these things are swept aside in favor of the all-important end, namely winning. To be elected becomes not a matter of mutual respect for the human dialogue but a matter of human engineering with the candidate and his staff being the engineers and the public little better than a material object to be molded and pressured this way and that.

One can go on enumerating various types of manipulation in the contemporary world: e.g., pressure in armies and navies, sometimes in schools, in scientific laboratories where fetuses are dissected and the sperm cells are stored for future impersonal insemination, in large corporations where employees are transferred from state to state and even from country to country, not just once in a lifetime but with a high degree of frequency so that no family roots can be put down. The list is endless.

The surprising thing is that deeply Christian, deeply apostolic persons sometimes can fall into the mentality and perhaps even into the habit of manipulation in an effort to promote the Gospel of Christ. This is often done unconsciously but yet with great damage to the authenticity of the Christian spirit and the Christian message. Who is not familiar, for example, with the clergyman who, not satisfied with the beauty and power of the Gospel words themselves, finds it necessary to hype them up with dramatic shouts and pauses, whispers and extravagant gestures? Or the preacher who lays such stress on the emotions of his listeners that they are thrown into a sort of hysteria which, on the lower levels of religion, can lead to wild dances and compulsive jerking and grovelling on the ground? Where is Christ in all this? This is no human response; rather the manipulative stirring up of the irrational passions totally at variance with the quiet, strong, serene freedom of response which is the normal fruit of Spirit-laden Christian preaching.

The over-zealous apostle in human relations only succeeds in alienating wavering, borderline Christians rather than returning them safely and solidly to the fold. Promising them human and earthly consolation which Christ Himself never promised and which indeed is very unlikely to be fulfilled in this world, or, on the other hand, frightening them with threats which Christ never uttered, especially to the poor and the ignorant and the misguided, these zealots, even if they do gain temporary success, can only succeed in the long run in weakening the visible posture of the Church in and to the world. People may give in for a time to importunities in order to avoid momentary embarrassments but once their freedom and poise are regained they are likely to turn even more strongly away from those who have "conned" them, either by threatening or seducing. The Church was built up under Christ by men and women who, by simple, direct Christian lives and preaching, brought the enlightenment of God's truth and the power of His grace to their fellowmen as a gift to their freedom and not as a means to enslave them. This was the way it had to be; the Great Redeemer by definition comes to make men free.

It is true that there is often a fine line between manipulative propaganda and authentic teaching. But the key questions to ask are these: "Is this teaching presenting truth in its integrity and does it present it in such a way as to reveal respect for human intelligence and concern for human liberty?" "Is it teaching of a type that sets up a mutually respectful dialogue or is it forced training such as one would expect Pavlov to administer to his dogs?"

The same questions apply to *persuasion*. In its legitimate sense persuasion makes a genuine and well-founded appeal to human motivation in such a way as to leave the person free to come to a truly human decision based on the proper priority of values. The more persuasion dehumanizes its object by diminishing the freedom and the responsibility of the response, the more it becomes mere manipulation. Christian witness, teaching, persuasion are quite otherwise. They reaffirm the dignity of the person on the deepest levels of wisdom and freedom.

7.

AUTO-SUGGESTION

Many persons of the older generation will remember the Coué fad which swept the world in the early part of this century. In its simplest form, this theory, based on auto-suggestion, seemed to imply that persons could improve themselves by a constant suggestion to themselves that they were getting better and better each day. "Everyday in every way I'm getting better and better." Some no doubt found the system helpful, but in its popular form it apparently was too vague and superficial to achieve the results which had been anticipated in the publicity.

Today however there is a revival of the same principle in new forms. Auto-suggestion has caught on once again, to some extent in transcendental meditation but especially in the semi-scientific process known as bio-feedback. Related in a generic way to the famous lie detector, the bio-feedback machine records various changes in the blood pressure, in tension and particularly, so it is claimed, in the brainwaves. The individual can monitor his own state of distraction and tension through the sound of beeps or other measuring devices. With a bit of attentive practice one can develop the ability to lower these tensions to a point where the machine records easy-going waves, signifying a relaxed condition. It is difficult to explain how this operates scientifically but it would seem that it is simply a form of auto-suggestion aided and reinforced by the use of a registering device which, somehow or other, seems to expand one's ability to control his so-called automatic functions. It seems that the machine is simply a psychological aid which helps to focus the concentration of the subject in the direction of minimizing the disturbing factors within himself.

Transcendental meditation, without the use of mechanical devices, has been known to achieve similar effects. Once again the mechanics of the process are somewhat mysterious but the desired alpha waves of the brain are reinforced and expanded through the meditative process, creating a soothing and restful bodily and mental condition.

Whatever one may think of these particular methods they have served to remind us that we are capable of a great deal more control of our minds and bodies then we might have believed in the past. This has great significance on the moral and spiritual levels as well as on the other levels already mentioned. Let us examine one or two of the possibilities.

On the moral level a person may be greatly bothered by sensual temptations of one kind or another, whether of gluttony, lust, sloth or the like; he may find that he is being thrown into a constant state of disturbance by having to wrestle with these temptations. A sort of warfare goes on, which leaves the tempted person exhausted, distracted, and often on the verge of despair, if he is devout and desires to lead a truly Christ-like life. Of course, he may use the normal means to counter these temptations such as prayer and positive courses of action, but even in spite of these excellent measures he may find the intrusion of the temptation at the most unexpected and often the most undesirable moments. It is as though his unconscious or sub-conscious is waging a warfare against his peace of mind, offering continuous distractions, unremitting allurements away from the paths he would follow. What other steps can he take, in addition to those already mentioned, that may be helpful in the solution of his difficulties?

If the so-called temptation has reached a point of such compulsive strength that it has the clear marks of a neurosis, then professional psychological help may well be in order. But on the assumption that the condition has not attained that degree of gravity, the use of auto-suggestive techniques in the context of Christian faith may well offer considerable alleviation.

So, too, in the matter of prayer itself. Many persons are devoted to their prayers but find that these prayers are largely a series of continuous distractions and that thus the normal expectation that prayer will bring peace and strength to the soul is often frustrated and even counteracted. Prayer may in fact lead to deeper distresses, deeper spiritual distraction than would have been the case had the prayers not been undertaken. Once again Christian auto-suggestion may be helpful.

Of what does this auto-suggestion consist? It may consist of a person's simply suggesting to his mind and emotions and body that they contribute to a calm atmosphere so that he may pursue the positive spiritual goals to which he is called by the Lord. He suggests that the pursuit of these goals is for the good of his whole person on every level. All levels stand to benefit by the fulfillment of God's will in Christ. For any level to resist the others in this matter is in the long run to be self-defeating. He tells himself that the previous chaotic condition of his mind and heart has not benefitted any part of his being and therefore that it will be highly desirable that all elements cooperate for the good of the whole and for the good of each individual element.

The person makes the suggestion to himself seriously, slowly, profoundly. He repeats the suggestions at least once a day, perhaps more often. He tries to draw his whole being into an awareness of the implications of his suggestion. Finally as time goes on and some results are obtained, however slight, he may give himself words of encouragement, commending his unconscious self for its cooperation and expressing the hope and desire for even greater achievement.

The tone of the suggestion is highly important if good results are to be achieved. The individual does not bark commands at himself. He does not denigrate himself. This type of ruthless self-dealing may often be at the very root of the problem which he is trying to solve. The unconscious, the sub-conscious, and even the physical substratum of the person often tend to be laws unto themselves and resent overbearing treatment by the conscious ego. The more the conscious issues commands in a dictatorial tone the more the lower levels may resist. On the other hand, experience has shown that a "respectful", "sympathetic", "reasonable", suggestion to the lower levels of human nature may often result in a surprisingly constructive response. In our day-to-day experiences with others we are well aware that suggestion is not the same as command. We are much more likely to cooperate with a polite suggestion rather than with a ruthless command. The same seems to be true within that extraordinary complex known as the human person.

This type of auto-suggestion becomes especially effective when it is undertaken in a spirit of faith in God's power to heal and to reconcile. The subject asks God to reinforce his suggestions to the various levels of his own personhood so that these suggestions may permeate every corner of the unconscious, every aspect of one's total nature. And the subject enlists the cooperation of his total being not primarily for himself alone but for God's saving purpose, to which the whole created nature is called. St. Paul proclaims in Romans that all nature groans and travails up to now until it be taken up in the freedom of the sons of God.

8.

INTERIOR RECONCILIATION

A follow-up on the chapter on Auto-Suggestion would lead us to reflect more deeply on self-hatred as the cause of moral and spiritual disorder and therefore on the need of valid self-love if the Christian life is to be lived out authentically.

Present-day psychologists and psychiatrists are relentless in issuing books and pamphlets on the disastrous effects of self-hatred. Some of these writers go too far in the sense that they would eliminate every concept of guilt, every interior pressure for self-reform or correction. But despite certain extremes by certain writers the general theme of the destructive power of self-hatred is well taken. Hating himself, the individual tends to project this same hatred on others and hence lives in an atmosphere of alienation not only from himself but from everyone else. This self-hatred may also reveal itself in a type of apathy which, while not notable for any overt or hostile actions toward others, is essentially an alienated state because the individual feels himself incapable of constructive accomplishment and therefore is unwilling to risk social relationships.

Psychiatrists are fond of telling us case histories. One can reflect, for example, upon the case of John X, who, as a child, was constantly put down by his parents. For one reason or another he was made to feel that he was almost worthless. Being unable to vent his consequent wrath on his parents, he could only vent it on himself as the one responsible for not making a greater impression on those who might have wished to love him. As time goes on, every negative experience tends to reinforce this early self-hatred because it reminds the individual of his non-goodness, thus stimulating his anger once again. If no one else is available to vent it upon he vents it to himself either by interior tongue-lashings or by actual physical torment such as excessive fasting or undertaking tasks beyond his power or some other form of acting out his self-disregard.

Psychiatrists point out that when one's self-hatred reaches a deeply neurotic stage it can very well lead to suicidal impulses and perhaps even actual suicide. If this is true in the physical order it can be equally true spiritually, sometimes even apart from the state of deep neurosis. A person may develop a state of mind whereby he feels himself hopeless in the eyes of God and man and thus gives up the fight to live morally or prayerfully. Then his self-hatred leads him to plunge more and more deeply into a state of alienation from God and man by repeated sinful acts, repeatedly destructive conduct. But he attains no real happiness from this because his self-recrimination has become even more profound.

These are extreme cases, of course, but even the moderately self-hating person may, while retaining the state of grace, make the Christian life so difficult for himself that it becomes almost insupportable. People of this type are often scrupulous, having so little respect for themselves or confidence in their morality that they are ready to accuse themselves of sin for the most superficial and inappropriate reasons.

And perhaps even more importantly, their manner of dealing with their temptations is calculated to increase their tempting power. By their attempts directly to throttle temptation they often give them a strength and importance which they otherwise would not have had. Concentration is centered on the destruction of the evil motion but unfortunately the evil motion is enhanced precisely by concentration upon it. Moreover the inherent stubbornness deep down in human nature on every level leads the lower tendency to resist more forcefully indiscreet and overbearing efforts to quench it. As indicated in the chapter on Auto Suggestion, lower movements are not necessarily evil in themselves but they need to be reoriented, reconciled with the general good of the person in whom they inhere. Thus the solution is not self-hatred but reconciliation—positive reconciliation of the sometimes conflicting elements within one's being. In Christian terms this reconciliation can be accomplished through faith, through prayer, and through auto suggestion permeated by both.

Here perhaps it is well to reflect on the Christian responsibility to love oneself. God loves every human being and therefore He loves the individual in question. The individual must love what God loves, including himself. Not only that. He has a responsibility to protect himself, to perfect himself and to attain the end for which God created him. This obviously demands self-love, self-concern, self-valuing. And this self-love has a very special significance and dimension in Christian terms because through baptism and grace one becomes a son of God, a temple of the Holy Spirit, therefore united with God in a way which demands not only natural but supernatural charity. All this seems obvious enough in theory but many good Christians and even some of the Saints at times have revealed a somewhat morbid type of self-hatred which is not warranted by the Gospel.

It might be objected that Jesus demanded of His disciples that they deny themselves, take up their cross and follow Him, and that this command implies a type of self-hatred. The obvious answer is that self-denial is not necessarily self-hatred. In fact, in Christian terms what is involved here is an authentic setting of priorities. A person is called upon to seek his highest good and thus to bring the other levels of his being in harmony with that highest good, for the good of the whole. His denial of certain aspects of himself involves not a rejection of his nature but a reorientation of it, a reconciliation of it in a higher synthesis.

It is also true that Jesus speaks of hating this world, even one's family, even one's own life, of dying to oneself, etc., but once again all these statements must be viewed in the light of the new and higher life which is offered to the soul living in union with Christ. The term hatred in these contexts does not refer to the destructive emotion of hate but the unwillingness to be dominated by merely human persons and convictions. It is concerned with the appropriate setting of priorities, the putting of God and His will before all things but with the realization that God then restores all things harmoniously and with a value that they did not have before. It may be summarized by the familiar words: "Seek ye first the kingdom of God and His justice and all these things shall be added on to you." In order to do God's will a person may indeed be required to sacrifice the company of loved ones and even his own ambitions, perhaps even his own life, but all these things will be restored in a new perfection in the synthesis of eternal life. This is not a matter of self-hatred in the psychological sense but of purely loving oneself in God and God in oneself.

The Christian who meditates on the difference between Christian self-love and pathological self-hatred will readily come to understand the warm and positive approach he must take with his own interior conflicts. His concern will be to harmonize, to reconcile, to reorient his interior elements and proclivities in such a way that his total person may move toward God. This is truly good for him as a whole even though it may not be immediately experienced as good on every level. But in harmonizing the tendencies and energies of his total nature in a context of Christian priorities the Christian will find the aiding power of grace and the strengthening of motivation which comes from "acted-out" faith. The goal of inner unity will sooner or later reveal itself as a blessing to the person's lower as well as to his higher nature.

9.

TO WHOM SHALL WE GO?

Surely one of the most touching incidents in the Gospel occurs in the sixth chapter of St. John, where we are told that even some of Christ's disciples could not see their way clear to accepting His teaching on the Eucharist and therefore "walked with Him no more." Jesus turned to those that remained and asked, "Will you also go away?" The response of St. Peter has resonances for every age, particularly for our own: "Lord, to whom shall we go? Thou hast the words of eternal life. For we have come to know and believe that Thou are the Christ the Son of God."

Unfortunately the first part of this scene has been repeated innumerable times in our own day. Everyone knows some Catholic, perhaps many, who have given up active commitment to and participation in their faith for reasons even more tenuous than those of the defecting disciples. As everyone knows, this trend is particularly noticeable in teen-agers and young adults although it is not confined wholly to them.

Their reasons, it would seem, are usually vague, imprecise. They are against institutional religion, or they find the moral code of Christ's church too rigid, or they can't buy the other-worldliness of the Christian teachings, or they find it too difficult to maintain faith in such supernatural doctrines as virgin birth, incarnation, resurrection, hell and the like. Interestingly enough you rarely hear any objection voiced to the doctrine of the Eucharist.

One wonders, however, whether these people realize all that they are giving up. Have they perhaps been living on the surface of the faith, conscious of rules and demands and outward structure but failing to appreciate the deeper significances of the Christian life of faith and grace? One would think that it would be very difficult for persons of sensitive understanding to abandon the notion of God redeeming, of the saving and transforming presence of Christ as the servant in his Church, or His in-dwelling presence in the individual, or the warming, ennobling and transfiguring power of His love penetrating one's heart and indeed the very depths of one's being. You wonder whether such persons could ever really have experienced the sense of God's nearness in the Church, in their brothers, and especially in the Eucharist. Does the healing power of Christ, His merciful renewing forgiveness, mean nothing to them? Amazement can be the only response to their disregard of what it means to be called by Christ to a way of life that gives new dimension to even the most trivial activity of the day. It does not seem possible that their private apostate reasonings could stand up against the profound Christian thinking and living and worshipping of two thousand years.

The defecting disciples had perhaps not seen Christ in the fullness of His saving action or understood the sublime profundity of His doctrine or grasped the divine reality of His power and authority. But that was two thousand years ago. After the epiphanies of all these years it is hard to see how Catholics nurtured in the faith can walk away from Christ so easily.

There must be great difficulties, one would think, in turning one's back on the miracles, the missions, the martyrdoms, the unremitting charities, not to mention Mary, the angels and the saints, the holy people, and even the sinners who have never lost faith, who have always preserved hope. The faithful Christian mind is almost overwhelmed by the fact that so many nominal followers of Christ have so casually abandoned the joyous life of sonship with its profound meaning and its life-enhancing gifts here and to come.

These defections would perhaps be somewhat less puzzling if

the defectors turned away to some form of life which seemed to offer equivalent promise. But in fact, as far as observation can determine, they have abandoned life in Christ's mystical body for empty, shallow, ultimately unrewarding attitudes or forms of existence.

What does the teenager gain when he abandons his faith and gives up his religious practice? In exchange for all that we have mentioned he now finds himself thrown wholly on his own devices, his own sensations, his own quirks and impulses. Many seemingly turn to dope or to continuously lecherous conduct or to a sort of sullen rebelliousness which offers nothing but unhappiness to them and to others. Is their ego enhanced, their spirit of independence? After a couple of years of this type of life they will be the first to admit their own frustrations, their own sense of the absurdity of life.

But what of the more religious-minded who turn from Christ to Zen, to a Guru, to oriental mysticism, or to so-called mind-expanding psychological routines? Once again the end product seems to be a sort of emptiness which, although it may be accompanied by a certain quieting of nerves and an elimination of anxiety, seems actually to offer no solid content, no God reality, no religious truths which have the power to give meaning to every phase of life and, most basically, to human existence itself. Apathy is often mistaken for calm and peace while the deep need of the human heart for a personal saving God can find no authentic answer either in free-flowing meditative exercises, in the words and actions of a guru, however benign and penetrating, or in the psychological gimmicks of various types of group therapy. What a poor exchange for the richness of the Christian life!

Others, no doubt because of their bad marriages, or their birth control, or their abortions, or their general spiritual laziness, find it more convenient not to walk with Christ any more. Some do have deep resentments against priests or other members of the Church and find their revenge in defection. It does not take them many years, one suspects, to find themselves drudging along with a certain spiritual hopelessness and dullness which can never compensate for what they have lost. Fortunately many of these try to live at least a compromise form of Christianity, responding to those parts of the Gospel which they find convenient or inspiring. There is hope that their faith may not be completely dead.

Perhaps there are some sincere apostates who think that they do a service to God by their defection. But even for them, the question still remains: "To whom shall you go?" Is there a philosophy or a religion or a way of life which can offer what the life of the Church offers to those who live it out sincerely? Even on a pragmatic basis, defection from the Church is a disaster for those who leave. When in human history have so many given up so much for so little?

This is one of the mysteries of our time, one of the great tragedies of the second half of our century. The answer, in human terms at least, seems to lie in a more effective witness to Christian truths and Christian values by those who have been gifted with an enduring faith. There is still, of course, the chance that pearls may be cast before swine. But it is more charitable to think that the millions of Catholics who have so cavalierly thrown their faith away in our times would not have done so if they had possessed deeper understanding of Christian doctrine, wider experience of Christian grace.

Perhaps Christ's remaining disciples must continue to shout from the house tops: "To whom will you go? He has the words of eternal life. You can come to know and to believe that He is Christ the Son of God."

10.

TOO MUCH, TOO SOON

Have you ever met anyone who complained that too much was expected of him by his employer, or, in the case of young people, by their parents? Something of the same sort can happen in the area of religious commitment, particularly when those making the demands are insensitive to the limitations of those under them. But even where such insensitivity is lacking, the drive for perfection which is necessarily inherent in the Christian faith can sometimes seem overwhelming to those who are only too aware of their frailties and their limitations.

Spiritual writers quite naturally (or supernaturally) usually shoot for the stars in their writing. Obviously they are not going to recommend a mediocre Christian life. They are busy encouraging people to be saints, stirring them up to surpass themselves, to grow toward the fullness of Christian holiness. Robert Browning had something of this thought in his familiar words: "Man's reach must exceed his grasp else what's a heav'n for?" It would seem that the pursuit of perfection must always leave us a little dissatisfied, a little more conscious of our incapabilities. This is no doubt good for our humility and often leads us to throw ourselves into the heart of Christ and ask Him to carry us along to wherever He chooses to take us.

However, for most of us, certain elements of uneasiness about our failure to come up to the mark seem to persevere and to grow as the demands upon us increase. Parishioners in an active parish know this feeling very well. They find it morally and even physically impossible to belong to all the appropriate societies, to support all the manifold activities, to contribute generously to all the various collections, to attend all the special services, to be promoters of social action in their community, to be involved in the adequate Christian education of their children and at the same time to lead lives of high personal sanctity in every phase of their relationships. They are inclined to cry out with Shakespeare's character: "Hold, enough!"

Nor are the clergy immune from these feelings of frustration. Not only are they expected to plan, to lead, and to implement the multitudinous projects of the Church, but at the same time they are expected to be shining exemplars of Christian faith, hope, and charity to an almost heroic degree. The parish priest sometimes has the impression that he is being drowned in exhortations from his superiors to preach sublimely, to counsel untiringly, to promote works of charity without limit, to visit the sick endlessly, to instruct the ignorant superbly, to build up the kingdom unceasingly and to provide infinite avenues of salvation and of sanctification for every member of his parish, at the same time practicing poverty, chastity, and obedience resplendently. No wonder there is a tendency to achieve a state of mental and spiritual compromise where fresh demands are not taken too seriously and a man tells himself that he can only do "the best that he can."

If the well-meaning Christian, whether lay or clerical, admits only the level of compromise just described, his case is indeed far from hopeless. But the danger is that unthinking or excessive demands will lead to far worse reactions which may be destructive of the Christian life at its very roots.

We all know how a child reacts when he is over-extended by his parents or teachers. The response of adults is not much different. If you give a child heavy tasks which he feels to be beyond his strength, he may try to carry them out if he possesses very good will but his constant failures will lead him to a state of discouragement. Then he may give up every effort to do what is expected of him. Or if this is not the case he will at least develop an attitude of apathy, of going through the motions simply to please his parents or teachers, without any real hope of accom-

plishment. In fact he may even lose the desire for accomplishment
since he cannot help but feel that if he succeeds in this task new
ones may well be added. If, as sometimes may happen, new tasks
are superimposed upon what he already finds difficult the spirit
of rebelliousness may begin to develop apace. Then the apathy
will be transformed into positive resistance and even contrary
actions. His mind and emotions will be tainted by a sense of injustice, a sense of resentment at the lack of understanding of those
in authority over him. This can result not only in present unhappiness and disruption in the home but in future tragedies of alienation. The seeds may be sown for a future crisis of devastating
proportions.

But even barring active rebelliousness, a spirit of cynicism is
almost certain to develop. The parents or teachers "don't understand, they don't care, they're only looking for their own ends."
They are manipulative, despite all the overt declarations of concern for the individual's human dignity and welfare.

Such cynicism is deadly in many areas but particularly in the
spiritual, where an innocent sincerity is almost the hallmark of
the committed Christian.

We have been speaking of moral demands, but the same principles apply in the area of teaching and indoctrination. There is
a time for everything and sometimes the time is not yet. Christ
Himself acknowledged this when He told His apostles, on one
occasion at least, that they were not ready for some profound
teachings which He had yet to communicate. Quoting from the
Old Testament, He also warned against bruising the tender reed
and quenching the smoking flax, as though to tell us that, in
Christian terms, people must be met where they are, with all their
limitations, and not be crushed by more than they can bear. And
lest anyone think that he might be able to bear the burden of the
Gospel alone, He also warned that "without Me you can do
nothing."

St. Paul, who also spoke of the unsuitability of giving strong
meat to babes who need milk, expressed in a reverse way the
above teaching of Christ: "I can do all things in Him who

strengthens me." The assumption was, it would seem, that growth in Christ and total confidence in Him would be needful for the fuller understanding and carrying out of the Christian life.

Moreover, when we view the Bible as a whole we see a gradualism that takes deeply into account the limitations of human nature. The whole Old Testament is a step by step revelation of the mind of God and of the sublime possibility of holy living. The whole leads up to the coming of Christ who in turn instructs His disciples gradually and makes graduated demands upon them until they receive the fullness of the Holy Spirit on Pentecost. He was careful to see that they were not called upon for too much, too soon, although never by any means did He propose to them a mediocre form of Christian life.

Perhaps the contemporary Christian can learn something from meditation on these themes. He can learn that although the highest is expected of him he is not expected to attain the highest in an instant. He will recall Newman's words, "one step enough for me." One step (even a baby step) at a time will traverse a long distance if consistency is maintained. The "little way" made popular by St. Therese could be a possible route for those who feel incapable of giant steps or multitudinous projects.

The contemporary Christian will recognize that he is called to perform works and to attain goals beyond his human powers. Having recognized this, he will not be discouraged, because he will not depend on his own powers. He will place himself in the hands of God, enlisting His strength, then do what he can and leave the rest to Providence.

In the area of understanding he may come to realize that total insight into the Christian message is not attained even by the greatest doctors of the Church and therefore is not to be expected of the rank and file. He will welcome each glimmer of light and realize that a life-long task of insight awaits him, yet a task which rewards each new flicker of understanding with another.

He will come better to appreciate that the Christian life is an ongoing pilgrimage often up hill and always with the goal lying brightly on the horizon.

11

THE FAITH OF YOUR CHURCH

Of the many striking expressions in the Mass liturgy, one which has a special resonance in the minds of many persons, is contained in the prayer to Christ shortly after the "Our Father," when the priest petitions the Lord to look "not upon our sins but upon the faith of Your Church." In a time when faith is so widely and deeply challenged there is a certain comfort and strength in turning to the solidarity of Christian belief which depends not just on this or that individual but on the historic community of the Church persisting over two thousand years and now still making its profession before the world. In faith, as in all other things in the Church, the individual does not stand alone. He stands with God and Christ and in the mystical body of Christ with his fellow cells and members. He marches not alone but in the great band of the people of God. Although such an idea is axiomatic, it seems often to be forgotten, particularly in the area of faith, where all too often the individual is depicted as standing in isolation against all the forces of intellect, science, and history which may be mustered against his beliefs.

This picture of the person alone, gritting his teeth and hanging on by a thread to his faith in the midst of scandal, temptations, and apparent contradictions has unfortunately been a common misrepresentation both in literature and in life. Indeed this isolating technique has even succeeded in convincing large numbers of

Catholics, not to mention other Christians, that they stand or fall by themselves, and that thus they must be able to defend themselves against every line of attack. Such an illusion places an impossible burden on the individual. How can one person, however brilliant and well-meaning, give adequate answers to all the multitudinous objections which can be directed against his holy religion? The very nature of Christianity, since it embraces the deepest mysteries of human life, both natural and supernatural, and intertwines itself with and permeates every phase of living, is such that it offers a limitless target for the arrows of its enemies.

Yet many modern Catholics have apparently been brain-washed into thinking that if they do not have an adequate answer to this or that objection or indeed if they themselves are puzzled by some aspect of Catholic teaching, they have failed their faith or perhaps their faith has failed them. Often without even attempting to go beyond themselves in formulating answers, they become so frustrated and embarrassed by difficulties that they regard themselves as "losing the faith." The fathers, the doctors, the scholars, the saints, the martyrs, the everyday believers of two millenia seem to have nothing to offer them when they are confronted with challenges to their faith. Seemingly unable to stand the gaff alone, they give up the most precious thing, the most precious Person, in their lives and, like the dissidents described in St. John's Gospel, "they walk with Him no more." All too often they do not remember the words of the liturgy: "Look not upon our sins but upon the faith of your Church."

It is true that St. Peter exhorted the Christians of his time to have "a reason for the hope that is in you" and that the Church has always encouraged its members to have the deepest possible understanding of the realities of faith. But certainly it was never contemplated that any private individual would have a ready answer for everything, much less that he could support and nourish his faith in an atmosphere of isolation. The very nature of the Christian brotherhood has always meant a mutual supportiveness not only in virtue but in the understanding of a common tradition and set of scriptures at whose wells the whole Christian people

were to drink. If one individual could not answer an objection
against faith, then there are always others who would be better
equipped. If they failed, then there were the official tradition and
magisterium of the Church as well as the writings of the fathers,
the doctors, the theologians, and the spiritual authors. Most of all,
there was the Holy Spirit of Truth Himself, at work primarily
and principally in the Church as a whole, enabling her to deal
with difficulties appropriately and to propound doctrines contained either explicitly or implicitly in Scripture and tradition.
It was never thought that an individual was professing a private
faith which he whittled out for himself, but that by his commitment to the Church he was entering into "the faith of your
Church."

Such thoughts tend to relieve the private pressures against
faith experienced by so many well-meaning Christians today,
when they seem unable to cope with the avalanche of objections
to and criticisms of their belief. One can imagine the Catholic
who takes the words of the Mass seriously, saying: "I do not
know the answer to this difficulty and I am perfectly willing to
admit that it seems almost overwhelming. I further admit that I
do not personally know all the subtleties, the nuances of Catholic
teachings on the very point which is under fire. But this will not
cause me to give up my faith in the doctrine. I know that the
objection has been answered or is being answered or will be
answered appropriately by the Spirit working in the Church. I
know that my limitations as a theologian or even as a simple member of the faithful, with a limited grasp of Christian doctrine, are
supplemented and supported by the whole vast tradition of divinely illuminated teaching and insight. If God wills, I intend to
look into the subject more deeply in a way that is suitable to
my intelligence and state in life, but I will not suspend or with-
hold my faith for a moment. I ask the Lord to 'look not upon my
sins but on the faith of His Church'."

Although it may be argued in contravention that each person is responsible for himself in terms of faith as well as every
other virtue, the fact is that the Catholic belongs to a body of

people, to a brotherhood, and that his knowledge of Christ and his commitment to Him are brought about through this body, in the midst of this body, and with the continuing support of this body. Indeed he would not possess the Catholic faith unless it had been communicated to him by the Catholic Church. His faith is a communal faith, interpreted in the community of faith, and not a private guessing game with God.

His private responsibility lies in his willingness to share in a belief which is greater than the mind of any individual believer and which finds its strength and clarity precisely in the commonality of the teachings guaranteed by the Spirit within the Church as a whole. It is because he experiences Christ in Christ's mystical Body, the Church, and not in some private mysticism, that he is enabled to take his lasting place in a community of faith. Against such a background, the significance of the English translation of the creed becomes strikingly evident: "*We* believe."

Unless I am baptized into the Church, unless I have the Gospel preached to me by the Church, unless I am enriched by the sacramental and supportive charitable life of the Church, unless I am drawn into the communion of saints, how can I believe, how can I live as a Catholic individual? Because of this saving brotherhood of Christ, through the power of the Spirit I can repel every doubt and in fact grow in peaceful belief by uttering the words of the liturgy: "Look not upon our sins, but upon the faith of Your Church."

12.

SWEET MYSTERY OF LIFE

Someone said recently: "You Christians and particularly you Catholics love to use the word 'mystery' as a cop-out for the contradictions and absurdities of your religious faith. Someone asks you to explain the Trinity and you answer by saying that it is inexplicable because it is a mystery. That seems to settle the question for you, if not for the person inquiring. Observers all along the line feel that if you cannot answer a question intelligently you invoke the concept of mystery to get you off the hook. I'm sorry to say that such answers won't do in a scientific age. Science has taught us to probe everything to its depth and to have confidence that a solution will ultimately be found if it is not presently available."

One might be tempted to comment on the "mysterious" faith of such individuals in the power of "science," but it is probably true to say that most great scientists have always recognized the limitations of their discipline, have always known that there were factors not subject to microscope, telescope, rules of mathematics or any other known form of measurement. The rationalism of the eighteenth century now seems somewhat absurd itself, tending to limit human horizons rather than to expand them, tending to regard a limited creature like man capable of attaining infinite knowledge by his own unaided efforts.

But there is also an anti-rationalist trend which in some ways may be equally deplorable. Someone else said recently: "The Christian Church, particularly the Catholic Church, has lost much of its appeal for genuinely religious people. By using the vernacular in the liturgy, for example, it removes the whole atmosphere of awe and mystery which made the Mass such a transcendental experience for many. Then there is the constant modern tendency to explain away the mysteries of the faith, particularly the mysteries of Scripture as mere myths which were intended to serve as analogues for rather commonplace naturalistic human experiences. This de-mythologizing has stripped the infancy narratives of the gospels of almost every element of divine intervention; it has even been inclined to minimize Christ Himself to a point where His knowledge, and even His self-knowledge, were supposedly quite limited, the former being little more than that possessed by many of the rabbis of his time. I could go on and on but the point is in little need of additional proof: strip the Church of its mystery and you strip it of all that is most valuable in it."

Our purpose is not to mediate a debate or to enter into polemics. Both sides no doubt have elements in favor of their respective positions. That the Church has always used reason to its fullest possible power hardly needs proof to anyone who has studied the scholastic tradition, the tradition of the Fathers and even the Scriptures themselves. But that the Church has always proclaimed that there are elements of mystery in God, in His revelations, and in creation is likewise incontestable. Scholasticism, which pushed human reason to its limits in explaining and interpreting the elements of the Christian faith, did of course make great strides but it was forced to conclude its researches with the classic words: "*Omnia exeunt in mysterium.*"

Even an average Christian, or indeed an average anyone, could without too much effort come to the same conclusion. How can a finite creation exist without an infinite Creator? And how can an infinite Creator be encapsulated in a finite mind? If these were possible then Man would be God, a point of view which is actually implicit in the rationalist belief. And what of the purpose of creation? Indeed how can we speak of purpose unless we also speak of someone who has a purpose? And then why should the world be this way rather than some other way? Why should a spiritual mind and will and personality inform the body of a satin-skinned ape and call itself a man? And why the indefinite number of stars and the millions of evolutionary years and the multiplicity of animal and plant forms and the endless struggle between man's higher and lower nature?

The questions go on and on and, as one probes more deeply, the mysteries do not diminish but increase. Not that some mysteries are not soluble as our knowledge increases, but the more we know, the more we come to realize, if we are humble-minded, that the mysteries pertaining to the infinite God are limited in their penetrability, except in as much as He chooses to reveal their nature to us.

Actually the fact of mystery should not be a source of dismay but rather of celebration. It means that we are not to be overwhelmed by the banal and the commonplace. It promises us an ever-expanding destiny filled with new surprises, new possibilities, new opportunities toward self-transcendence. Because there is an infinite mystery there are infinite resources which in one way or another can be made available to us. Because there is an infinite mystery there is a possibility of ever-widening love, ever-expanding truth. Because there is an infinite mystery we do not walk alone, and the trials and hazards of the moment are not necessarily final; there is always an opening out. This is true because such mystery does not pose itself as an obstacle or barrier but a sea of infinite depth, a sky of infinite height, a Being, personal, knowing, loving, drawing us ever more and more deeply without ever exhausting the reality contained.

To say then that all things are rooted in and oriented to mystery is not to cut off human growth but to make it possible. Hence the authentic Christian lives in hope, happily accepting mystery as the fourth dimension of human life. It is perhaps the most significant mark of Christian maturity to accept mystery without rebelliousness but rather with thanks. It can offer unlimited possibilities to the beggar starving in the streets of Calcutta, to the terminal cancer patient in the scientifically equipped hospital, to the king upon his tottering throne, or to the average man living out a humdrum existence in a world that seems to be all grays and blacks. To be resistant to the fact that there are insoluble mysteries in life is in a sense to desire life to be more burdensome than it is. Those who resist the mystery of the cross are fashioning for themselves a gibbet of despair.

But acceptance of mystery is not anti-intellectualism or obscurantism. We know what we know but we also believe what we believe. We seek to know more but we also seek to believe more deeply. The danger of negating mystery is that we become complacent with our knowledge and thus learn less than we can learn; we undermine the saving power of belief, which opens up ever new horizons into which knowledge itself may enter, provided that it does not attempt to usurp the role of the Deity, does not fail to understand its own limitations.

Despite what its critics may say, mystery is not contradiction. It is not against reason, for reason and mystery come from the same source. To say that mystery is above reason but not contrary to it is not a mere juggling of words but a sincere statement of the fact that man is finite, God infinite. But God does not contradict man; He creates him. God does not frustrate man but offers him fulfillment in the possession of the beatific vision, where man's enhanced possibilities of knowledge and love are rewarded in an eternal but never satiating feast of plenty.

"All things terminate in mystery." In some ways this statement is not as mysterious as it sounds; it simply and profoundly means that all things terminate in God.

13.

THE COURAGE TO BE JOYFUL

Not long ago there was an article in one of the Catholic magazines berating the clergy for their sermons on Christian joy. The author felt a sense of indignation at priests, with so few personal troubles of their own, telling people crushed by all sorts of burdens in life that they should be joyful and full of good cheer despite the harsh things that might happen to them. He considered such sermons not only inept but almost insulting, since the preachers seemed to think that all one had to do was to take thought upon it and one could immediately bubble over with Christian joy despite sickness in the family, the loss of a job, or the fact that the mortgage payment might be due. He suggested that the clergymen might be more effective in their sermons on joy if they had shared some of the cross carryings and crucifixions of the average person in today's world; they then might not be so ready to speak in a glib and superficial manner of the possibilities of having a joyful Christian heart in the midst of a continuing Calvary experience.

The article was not only a little bitter but somewhat confused. The author seemed to resent being told to be joyful even though the preacher, however inexperienced in suffering he himself might have been, might only have been quoting the words of the Man of Sorrows or perhaps of St. Paul, who was certainly no stranger to affliction. "Rejoice, again I say, rejoice," he said.

Authentic Christians have never viewed suffering and joy as opposites. Even the most youthful and naive preacher knows that men must take up their cross to follow Christ. The message conveyed by such sermons, however ineptly, is surely that the surprising and indeed paradoxical effect of Christian commitment, interiorly activated, is that one can smile through tears, that one can find joy at least at the topmost point of one's soul even while hanging on the cross. Such comforts are often not so small.

From this peak of the soul a radiance is cast on all that lies beneath, a strength is given, a hopefulness is imparted, an assurance is communicated that all things can work to good, therefore to joy, when God's will is sought and accomplished. One would suspect that St. Paul's call to rejoice is not merely a word of encouragement but an admonition. It is rooted in the very depth of our faith, in Christ's saving and affirming power, his victory over sin and death, and all that these things imply. To rejoice therefore is a crucial demand: one's response to it is a true index of one's depth as a Christian, one's faith, particularly one's hope and even more so, one's love.

Is this to say, then, that this joy does not come automatically, that one has to stir it up by reflection on the Christian elements? No doubt for the saints who have habituated themselves to joy and fearlessness even under the least promising circumstances, the reflective action is not so necessary, but for non-saints constant meditations are needed about our vocation as Christians and all that that implies. And especially we may find the need to meditate on the example of the Lord, who was also the Suffering Servant.

You can see that here there is a cutting across what might be described as the worldly view of joyfulness. To many the state of joyfulness is inconceivable without the absence of circumstances and factors which create pain. How can one be joyful, much less cheerful, if one's mother is dying of cancer, if the head of the family has just lost his job, if the country is going into a depression, if the world is at war, or if the papers are filled with crime and mayhem? One can always find reasons, many reasons, for not being joyful. This is particularly so, of course, if the person in question has a melancholy temperament.

All these negative factors simply drive home the point that joy in the Christian sense must often be consciously stirred up, at least for most of us. But this isn't easy, we are told. One can assent intellectually to the Christian justification of being joyful even in the midst of sorrow, but the emotions are another matter. They are not subject to such "rationalizing." They have their own laws, which are not necessarily those of the Christian Gospel.

True enough, but sooner or later, with proper influence, they usually come around, become reconciled to a person's usual way of thinking. And they also are not permanently immune from a bit of pressure from the will. And when the power of God is brought to bear through prayer the transformation can be quicker than one might expect.

However, there is also another factor which is often overlooked: an individual needs *courage* to be joyful in the midst of trials. Experience in the Christian life shows that virtues do not stand alone, any more than their subjects stand alone. One virtue supports another, even leads to another. If it is obvious that the summit cannot exist without the base, it is perhaps less obvious that courage is an intimate component of an authentic Christian cross-carrying joyfulness. Often I am not joyful because I have no heart for it. Lethargy created by sorrow and pain leave me weak. I am overwhelmed by the distractions and disturbances of unhappy, unfortunate circumstances. In such a state I cannot grab hold of joy even though the imperative of the Christian gospel may pass through my mind. I need a lower step to climb up to that peak. Or, if you prefer, a hand-hold. This is courage.

Courage is something I can understand in the midst of pain and adversity. The circumstances of suffering meet me directly on the level of fortitude; I already have much experience struggling along, reeling, staggering, yet grimly determined to carry on, despite everything. I feel challenged by the courageousness of so many others who have lived out various forms of martyrdom not only in the past but presently on every side, not only

Christians indeed but persons of every commitment. Emotionally, instinctively, on the deepest levels, I know that I must not give in, that I must overcome. But generally this is a grim, grunting, groaning business.

Could I not stir up my courage just one further degree? Mustering those gospel thoughts that go through my mind, could I not find the courage to climb one step higher to the level of Christian joyfulness? Perhaps I could stimulate myself by saying that gloominess and melancholy are forms of cowardice. It takes heart to be hearty. "Be of good heart, it is I."

After all, our problems are not usually as dramatic and as tragic as they sometimes are or as they could be. Once for a couple of years a timid priest acted as chaplain in a home for incurable cancer patients. The sisters were a cheerful lot. Indeed the patients had a sort of quiet joyfulness which might seem surprising under the circumstances. Perhaps they had seen a sign in one of the main rooms: "Smile. God loves you." At first such a saying might seem almost obscene: people died every day and suffering went on continually. Yet, by and large, no one was blubbering, feeling sorry for himself, or shrouded in indissoluble gloom. The atmosphere was in fact heavenly, or at least suitable to the anteroom of heaven. The chaplain soon recognized that he was the only person in the place who was guilty of low-spiritedness. It was quite a revelation to him, especially about the need for courage in the face of adversity, even other people's adversity. It took him a long time to realize that it takes a lot of *courage* to smile in adverse circumstances but that God does love us and His strength is not lacking if we open our hearts to Him.

To say that human beings are sometimes joyless and fearful out of sloth, apathy, or self-indulgence, may seem rather heartless but there is at least a grain of truth in the allegation. In a certain sense it is easier for many people to be gloomy, melancholy, dour than to rejoice, to be of good cheer. It takes courage to make the effort to be joyful. It is worth the effort.

14.

GOD SO LOVED THE WORLD

If you were asked what is the most beautiful sentence in the New Testament what would be your answer? The question is perhaps unfair and indeed there are many possibilities but no doubt high on the list would be the statement of Jesus in the 3rd chapter of St. John: "God so loved the world that He gave His only Son, that whoever believes in Him may not die but may have eternal life." Not only does this sum up the whole theology of the New Testament in the simplest and yet the most profound form, but it stresses elements which so much need to be stressed in every age, and perhaps particularly in our own. The notion of God's loving the world, which may seem obvious to dedicated Christians, is a stunning revelation to those who view God either as a relentless hangman type or who deny His existence because they cannot imagine a God Who would create a world in which human beings would be so miserable. Then of course there is the third view, that of those so filled with self-hatred that the notion that anyone loves them, much less God Himself, is a concept which shatters all their pre-suppositions and habits of thought and feeling. Yet to know that God loves one, no matter how wretched one may be, no matter how hateful one may seem, could and should be a source of healing of even the most destructive neuroses.

The statement of God's love for the world is stupefying even to the rigid moralists who, whatever their verbal assertions, are imbued with the idea that they alone can save themselves by their teeth-gritting efforts to perfect themselves in accordance with abstract moral laws. How challenging to be told that God's love manifests itself in the sending of His Son "that whoever believes in Him may not die but may have eternal life." The Son, then, and not one's own isolated efforts, becomes the source of salvation. Belief of course implies acceptance, responsiveness, but this in itself is made possible through His power, His Spirit. The center of emphasis shifts from self to God in Christ and, with this shift in emphasis, new powers, new dimensions, are opened up in the human heart and mind enabling them to transcend themselves, to enter into divine life through the grace which by its very definition is a gratuitous gift of God.

St. John goes on: "God did not send the Son into the world to condemn the world, but that the world might be saved through Him." As we meditate on these words the old fears and anxieties, the self-reproaches and the aura of meaninglessness and absurdity which may have surrounded one's conduct are swept away in the promise of mercy and of faith. This is a question not merely of being saved from sin, although that is in itself a tremendous gift. It is a question of having one's whole life, one's whole meaning, validated and transformed and lifted up into the life of the God-head. Accepting the Saviour through responsive belief means entering into the life of sonship whereby man is enabled to call God not merely the Creator but "Abba," that is, "Father," in the most profound sense.

This does not mean that there will not be trials but rather that one will find the strength to endure, to be crucified, and yet to rise again spiritually in this life, totally in the next. It is interesting that Jesus in introducing His proclamation of God's love for the world says: "Just as Moses lifted up the serpent in the desert, so must the Son of man be lifted up, that all who believe may have eternal life in Him." The Old Testament tells us that, when the Israelites were suffering from a plague of fiery serpents which stung them drastically, Moses fashioned a bronze serpent, perhaps on the form of a cross, and held it up for the people to gaze upon.

Those who looked upon it in faith were healed. So, those who unite themselves with Christ in His sacrifice, His oblation to the Father, placing their own sufferings in solidarity with His, looking upon Him, in other words, with a unifying faith, share in the salvation which He won through the cross. In the words of St. Paul, "With Christ I am nailed to the cross." This is only the first moment in the paschal mysteries, which open out to glorification: "Thanks be to God Who has given us the victory through our Lord Jesus Christ."

But if in responding in loving faith to God's saving love a person is redeemed, then turning away from this blazing vision must be the great sin which can lead to ultimate destruction. "Whoever believes in Him avoids condemnation, but whoever does not believe in Him is already condemned for not believing in the name of God's only Son." To turn away from the light, to resist the love, which seems an incredible posture, is the greatest tragedy of human history, a tragedy particularly evident in our own time. "The judgment in question is this: the light came into the world, and men loved darkness rather than light because their deeds were wicked."

We can see this sin of resisting the light among many Catholics of our time. Those, for example, who, although retaining the name of Catholic, refuse to participate regularly in the liturgy, refuse to accept the more demanding teachings of the Church, are obviously turning their back on the saving Lord. Why is it that the nominal Catholic refuses to participate in the liturgical life of the Church? Is it not very often because attendance at Sunday Mass means that a spotlight is thrown upon his own life, revealing its dark corners and demanding that they be swept and opened up fully to the light? If a man is doing his own thing contrary to the teachings of the Gospel, it must be a harrowing experience to unite himself with Christ and his fellow Christians in oblation to the Father each Sunday and to hear the pure and undefiled word of God preached from the pulpit. This would mean a constant reproach; so, all too often, he stays away from the light lest his own sinfulness be revealed, not so much to others as to himself. "Every one who practices evil hates the light; he does not come near it for fear his deeds will be exposed."

Perhaps this is the reason that so many of our young people have become "disenchanted" with the Church and have fallen away from Mass and the sacraments. Many of them, after all, have grown up in an atmosphere of pornography, of accepted lust, and may have found themselves burdened with corrupt habits as they entered the teen years. This together with the teenage pressure tending to validate rather than discredit the licentiousness of the atmosphere makes attendance at Mass and listening to the pure word of God a frightening and at times almost a nauseating experience.

Even apart from liturgical prayer, private prayer, since it seeks to establish contact with God and therefore with the light, becomes almost a psychological impossibility. Light reveals ways which are contrary to the Gospel and to the saving message of Christ. And some will not endure the crucifixion of repentance, the crucifixion which is implicit in embracing the crucified One. Hence the words of Christ, "God did not send the Son into the world to condemn the world, but that the world might be saved through Him," become for them not words of salvation but of negative judgment. "Men loved the darkness rather than light because their deeds were wicked."

What of the agnostics or the pagans who have never even been touched by baptism? Some will not look upon Christ, the author and finisher of faith, with loving, responsive belief; all too often, having heard of his saving power, they refuse to follow this call to life to where it leads. In a sense, one can say that the great sin of the unbelieving world is not so much its unbelief as its indifference to the light, its unwillingness to examine the claims of Christ and His Church. "He does not come near it for fear his deeds will be exposed."

God's call is clear: We must respond with joyful confidence in God's love for us as manifested in the saving acts of Christ; we must open ourselves more and more fully to His light, living fuller Christian lives of deeper faith by the power of His love within us.

15.

ENNUI

Some keen observers of human nature have stated that the greatest cross a person has to bear is not the critical tragedies of life such as sickness, suffering, loss of loved ones, loss of job, and misunderstanding, but the burden of boredom day after day, year after year, the feeling of an unfulfilled life of tasteless and rootless experience, with very little hope of improvement. This continuing lack of zest, this boringness of life, with all the subtleties that it involves is all the more devastating because it is not traceable to any one problem but seems to permeate all aspects of a person's life. In the case of a great tragedy the person knows what he is meeting; he is challenged in concrete terms and, even though he may suffer great pain, he realizes that there are certain steps that he must take to survive. In the case of ennui one is drowned in a sea of bland insignificance, so to speak; there seems to be nothing that one can seize hold of to change his condition. Nor is it a condition, like most sicknesses, that either deteriorates to a point of death or improves gradually. Boredom tends to go on and on, with brief temporary remission perhaps, but with an over-all permeation that seems inescapable. Life becomes blanc-mange, meal after meal, day after day: blanc-mange and nothing else.

The symptoms of boredom are easy to discern, although its causes are often beyond comprehension. The bored person finds life in general unappetizing. He does not seem to be able to stir up an enthusiasm which is more than momentary even for the worthiest causes. In fact he tends to resent worthy causes as cynical attempts to divert him from the real meanness of life. Moreover they fail to take into account his overwhelming fatigue, another symptom of boredom. He no longer seems able to make an effort; indeed he has no desire to make an effort in any phase of his life unless it be an effort to unburden himself of every possible challenge.

His work becomes routine, lacking in flavor. Even the prospect of future promotion seems to offer more responsibility with less in the way of human appeal. He cannot see his way to changing his line of work since this would involve efforts which he believes himself to be incapable of making. The most he can do is to float along on the sea of routine dullness.

His friends and relatives, although not hated by him, are seen as colorless personalities who have been drained already of whatever charm they might once have lent to his life. All their ideas have been explored, every conversation has been the subject of endless repetition, every possibility for fruitful dialogue has been run into the ground. "If only," he says to himself, "I had interesting people around me, with stimulating and original ideas, who could sympathize with my deepest longings and make me feel valuable and interesting!" He is incapable of making the effort to meet such people and so he goes on with the old listless conversation, the impoverished relationships.

Leisure, although he wants as much of it as possible, becomes a time not of stimulation but of stupor. He drugs himself with television or mindless literature or unenriching games and sports. There seems to be no growth or improvement. He has done everything and now does it once again, ever more reluctantly. He seems to have lost whatever gift of creativity he may have once possessed. He can think of no new ways to pass the time so as to provide deeply human satisfaction.

When this boredom attacks a man's spiritual life, religious writers refer to it as accidie. Like all boredom accidie involves disgust, apathy, and a loss of energy. There is in fact a certain hopelessness about it that may attack the supernatural virtues at their very roots. This ennui is then far more serious than mere boredom with one's work or one's leisure. There develops a distaste for the very Gospel itself, for moral teachings or liturgical services, even for the very thought of God. This in turn leads, when it doesn't lead to a loss of faith, to apathy, particularly in prayer. A sort of spiritual paralysis sets in whereby the individual loses the desire and, as he thinks, even the energy to make contact with the Source of Christian life. He is like a neon sign reading "Christ," but without being plugged in to the current. Hence there is also the loss of charitable action. The effort to serve, to sympathize, to reach out in love, to proclaim the Gospel in one form or another becomes too great. It is easier just to be carried by the waves of boredom and to float nowhere in particular, listlessly and with only the faintest hope that one will recover one's former enthusiasm.

This is obviously a state which can lead to ultimate disaster and therefore must be remedied as soon as possible. But ironically the very nature of boredom seems to preclude the efforts necessary to overcome it. The person afflicted by accidie, however, if he has not abandoned the faith entirely, at least retains that slight germ of hope which God in His good time may fructify into transforming life.

The first step in overcoming spiritual boredom is to realize that this germ, this ember, still remains. Just to reflect on this in itself may open one out to a little more life, to a little more brightness. No thought here of gigantic effort but only of slight groping toward fuller growth.

Even the bored person will not find it too much effort to reflect on the hidden values of his boredom. He can accept it and view it as a time when "the well" fills up, so to speak. That is to say that, even though the horizon seems gray and unrelenting and a dull listless rain falls incessantly in his life, the effect may be to allow him to re-gather his forces, to re-deploy his energies, just as in the cold barrenness of winter the fruitful spring is already implicit.

Secondly, his very dissatisfaction with the dullness of his spiritual life can be viewed as a sort of blessing in itself. He can come to realize that the weight of his accidie is pressing him, despite his lethargy, to find a way to break out, just as pressing a grape forces out its central contents. He can view his ennui as a period of preparation for an outburst of innovative ideas, an energetic renewal. Without too much effort, he can reflect on Christ's invitation to the apostles to come aside and rest awhile for purposes of renewal. Perhaps he will not find it too difficult to rest blindly, even unfeelingly, in the heart which Jesus described as meek and humble.

Then the weight of boredom may be lifted ever so slightly so that some form of forced action, however tenuous, may be carried out. The individual can tell himself that even though his heart is not in it, even though he derives no satisfaction from it, nor sees any value in it, he *will* act out, at least in small ways, the role of the concerned Christian. In fact he himself will make little effort but will allow Christ to act it out in him.

The results may be surprising. There is a healing value in an act of charity, which enlivens the giver as well as the receiver. "It is a more blessed thing to give than to receive."

Enforced action can thus lead to willing action. This in turn will open up new perspectives, reveal unrealized powers in oneself. The ennui may not yet be vanquished, but in the distance Christ can be seen walking on the waters.

16.

VULNERABILITY

Have you ever noticed how astounded some people are by personal illness, death in the family, or indeed by any substantial change which they themselves have not planned? One would think that by the time such persons had reached an adult age they would have grasped the fact that vulnerability, and indeed susceptibility to change, are part of the human condition and therefore not something to be surprised at. The really surprising thing is that people survive as well as they do in resisting illness and death and other unwelcome changes in their condition, for nothing can be more certain.

The illusion of continuity in the same or a better state seduces us all. Without thinking too deeply about it, the child assumes that the security of his home and family life will be preserved indefinitely. The average person does not, unless he be neurotic, give himself much opportunity to dwell on the possible sudden loss of his home, insurance companies and prophets of gloom and doom notwithstanding. The young man, not to mention the mature man, who does well in his job and feels at home in his work, goes along on the unspoken assumption that his fruitful endeavor will continue at least on the same level, and possibly on a higher level in good time. The happily married parents view their family with a certain sense of complacency, knowing of course that the youngsters will eventually grow up and leave the parental nest,

yet tending to put such thoughts at the fringe of their consciousness as though they were not seriously to be reckoned with. The
child has an occasional nightmare about the death of his mother,
but this is precisely what it is, a nightmare, and it is designated as
such by his consoling parents. The reality of such an event is
minimized to the point where it has no more substance than a
fictional story or a disturbing movie.

Then perhaps the break-up of the home, the loss of a much-
needed job, the assault of serious illness or accident, or even the
final crushing reality of death may make itself felt in the lives of
individuals who have been living wrapped in the cocoon of illu-
sionary invulnerability. The shock and surprise are unutterable
and may destroy not only mental health but even faith in God.

Have not these people always known that the human condition
is ever subject to tragic disturbance, that its nature is such that
it must sooner or later be destroyed, at least physically, by the
forces which surround or are inherent in it? Of course everyone
knows this theoretically but the existential reality is another matter. It takes many people a long, hard time to adjust to their
vulnerability and mortality.

While granting that the rules of earthly life involve vulnerability, one can ask why such a life was permitted by an all-loving
God in the first place. On this level we come face to face with the
mystery of suffering, the mystery of physical evil, not to mention
moral evil. The fact that vulnerability is a mystery means that
no one can give a fully satisfactory explanation, but we cannot
ignore the fall of man, the evil effects of the misuse of freedom,
or the preparatory nature of human life, to mention a few significant elements. Teilhard seems to find what is for him a satisfactory answer to pain, suffering, and death, in the very nature of
the evolutionary process, which is one of trial and error, pressing
always forward from the alpha to the omega point, a journey
which of its nature involves loss and gain, the shucking off of old
forms to develop new, the endurance of necessary frictions from
which the finely modelled human structure of the future emerges.
All this is plausible, but the question then arises: why the evolu-

tionary process? We are back once more to the mystery of earthly human life in its present form.

Sooner or later we have to ask ourselves why the human spirit with its capacity of unlimited understanding of truth and love of goodness is seemingly "trapped" in the limitations of the human body, which is vulnerable by the very fact that it is material and subject to time and place, with its many dependencies on such things as food, light and heat, for its very survival. Moreover, the earthly body by its very nature is made up of separable parts and therefore is subject to dissolution.

We then have to ask ourselves another question, which is in some ways the same question: why the body at all? If we answer that it is the means by which we are individuated one from the other, the means by which we communicate with one another, the means whereby we attain knowledge of the true, and beautiful and good, and whereby we act out our responses to this knowledge through creative love—we must still ask "the why" of vulnerability and if such vulnerability could not be removed. Could not the All Powerful God have made a world of invulnerable bodies which would not be at odds with the innate desires of the spirit to continue in joyful existence without the limitations of time and illness and death?

As Christians we know that, although God has not chosen to do this now, He has promised to do it in the future. Our despair and horror at our vulnerability can only be dissipated by our confidence in His promise that if we are faithful and true to the end we shall be conformed in eternity to the glory of Christ's resurrected body, when all tears shall be wiped away from our eyes. This mortality shall put on immortality. Vulnerability shall become invulnerability. "Thanks be to God Who has given us the victory through our Lord Jesus Christ."

17.

INSTRUMENTALISM

A priest recently recounted the following experience: "Some time ago I was asked to give a spiritual talk at the Foundation for Christian Living, which is located in town. As many people know, this is Dr. Peale's organization, which carries on the circulation of his pamphlets and books and the collection and acceptance of funds which are sent in to him as a result of his radio and television preaching. Many of our Catholic people work there, but my talk was to be directed to the whole group. Naturally this was something of a challenge and I couldn't very well steal Dr. Peale's thunder and speak about positive thinking in the Christian life. In searching about for a topic, however, I found myself returning again and again to an insight which had been growing in me for a long time.

"As the years have gone on, I have come more and more to see that one of the problems, not only of a pastor but of any Christian who has a sense of apostolic mission, is to open himself out more fully to the powers of Christ's Spirit and to eliminate elements in himself which block the effectiveness of God's work in him. This notion of 'eliminating' might have seemed in conflict with positive thinking but, of course, there can be no positive without some removal or weakening of negative elements. To put the matter succinctly, my conclusion, as the result of long experience, was that my ego was placing an enormous obstacle in the way of God's communication through me to others.

"Sometimes we may be guilty of over-zeal, whereby we distort things to make a point; and at other times our apathy makes the word of God seem weak and the grace of God seem unavailable. And at still other times we can be so eager, unconsciously perhaps, to strengthen our own image in the sight of others, to win the approval of those with whom we deal, that we give the impression of working for ourselves rather than for God in Christ. Unfortunately we don't always recognize this, but people have an uncanny way of sensing the pure from the polluted where religious matters are concerned.

"In preparing my talk, I readily perceived that the way to become more truly and more fully God's instrument was not to stamp out the ego or to eliminate one's personal gifts, much less their fervent exercise, but to open these things up more fully to God's influencing Spirit, to harness them as it were in His service rather than one's own. An effective tool or instrument in the material order does not lose its identity, but rather offers its nature and qualities to the fullest possible extent, to be most effective. But it is effective always within the context of the person using the instrument. A good instrument, while retaining its properties and powers and identity, is responsive to the user, serving His purposes rather than its own. The concept of Christian instrumentalism therefore is not a negative one but one which releases the full powers of the person, the full resources of his personality and talents, but not for their own sake, not for the individual's sake, but for the purposes intended by the Divine Mover.

"In reflecting on the scriptural texts from which this concept is derived I found special illumination and encouragement from the sayings of St. Paul: 'I live, now not I, but Christ lives in me' and 'Let this mind be in you which was in Christ Jesus.' When I become totally motivated and activated by the Spirit and mind of Christ then I need have no fears about the success or failure of my Christian endeavors. I have been fully open and responsive to Him and the results are primarily His, not mine—which is the way it should be in Christian terms. In such a context idle fears disappear because, if God is with me, who can be against me? And

I know from experience that with such a mentality my ability to communicate Christ to others, to influence them for their own good and for God's glory, is multiplied and expanded and even transformed in unforeseen ways. My own attitude becomes not less loving but more so, with His loving Spirit dominant, while at the same time I become more detached since what is at stake is not my own prestige, popularity or exalted image but the work which God chooses to do in me at this time. My motives therefore are purified; I am no longer trying to win a popularity contest or make a record for myself but to do a job for Christ inasmuch as He chooses to use me at this time, for the purposes He has in His mind.

"One cannot help but think of the words of John the Baptist: 'He must increase while I must decrease.' The paradox of apostolic action among Christians is that the more one is deflated in terms of his own self-interest and defenses then the more Christ operates in and through one, the more successful one becomes as a Christian apostle. When you are able to say 'I live, now not I, but Christ lives in me,' you will also be able to say in terms of spiritual success, 'Thanks be to God who has given us the victory through our Lord Jesus Christ.'

"Various analogies about instrumentality can offer some light on this important concept. The first one, that of the donkey, I used in my talk to Dr. Peale's employees. I mentioned to them that I had often been impressed by Chesterton's poem which describes the donkey on which Christ rode on Palm Sunday as being filled with joy at the fact that, through his efforts, Christ had ridden into the hearts of the people of Jerusalem. Without becoming overly sentimental, I find it somewhat captivating to think that Christ can ride into the hearts of people on the back of a donkey, such as myself. After all, He Who can raise prophets from the stones doesn't need very much of an instrument to effect his apostolic purposes. The donkey, young or old, handsome or ugly, weak or strong, as long as he is able to totter short distances, is capable of being caught up in sublime salvation events if Christ is His rider. And a prudent donkey will be careful not to try to draw the crowd's attention to himself but to present a suitable throne for the redeeming King. He is most satisfied when all eyes are on Christ and when Christ's presence is made possible by him.

"The second analogy is that of the clean window pane which allows the sunlight to enter the room. The sunlight is the important thing, the window only the medium through which it enters. The window has failed in its purpose to the degree that it is covered with dirt or distorted in its transparency. The less it attracts attention to itself, the better it is performing its work. But consolingly, it is true that even a dusty and whorled window pane can still admit some healing and strengthening illumination.

"Sometimes when I feel particularly empty of saving thoughts or enthusiasm or I lack a sense of the presence of God, I think of myself as a kettledrum, which, empty as it is, the great musician can nevertheless use to set the tempo of other lives, to encourage them to a great and victorious forward march. God can beat out a tune even on an empty kettle, if there is no kettledrum to be found. Even when I am feeling very worthless, I know that I am not useless if God chooses to make me His instrument.

"Of all these analogies I suppose that I prefer that of the donkey because it is the least inanimate in its implications. Being God's instrument does not mean that I am without my own emotions, my own tendencies, my own character and personality traits. It means actually that these are enhanced and given a transformed power which they never before possessed.

"All that I have tried to say is summed up in St. Francis' beautiful prayer which begins 'O Lord, make me an instrument of your peace'."

18

GOD WILL PROVIDE

Jon Stallworthy's biography of Wilfred Owen, the English poet who died in World War I, describes Wilfred's mother as having great confidence throughout her life that "God will provide." The author tells us that this assurance was not always a consolation to "her more practical husband." The maxim that God will provide has long been a favorite of many Christians. It is worth reflecting on whether or not the husband was really more practical than the wife.

Of course we have all had a thousand experiences of not obtaining what we prayed for, at least in precisely the terms in which we made the petition. There tends, therefore, to be a certain scepticism in the so-called "practical minded" about assuming that God will provide in all circumstances. The "practical minded" might say in effect: "Sometimes God will provide and sometimes He won't. It's better therefore not to take any chances, but to provide for yourself as best you can. Wear a belt and suspenders and take out all available insurance to cover every eventuality. Then, if God provides, fine; but if He doesn't, at least you may save something out of the mess."

This seems very sensible, very practical. But we must ask ourselves whether such an attitude is not damaging to God, a violation, in a sense, of the trust and confidence we should have in Him. Or is it just possible that God desires us to take this practical approach and not to presume on His assistance, at least not in the terms which we ourselves define?

The present writer certainly does not consider himself qualified to solve all the mysteries of prayers of petition and God's

way of answering them. Nor is he capable of defining exactly
when confidence becomes presumption or, on the other hand,
when the precise moment occurs at which lack of confidence is
equivalent to lack of hope or even to lack of faith.

In connection with the words "God will provide," however,
we can perhaps discern certain things which the saying does not
mean:

(1) Certainly it does not mean that when faced with normal
or even arduous tasks one can remain in passivity and fail to take
the necessary action to accomplish what is actually within one's
own given powers. After all, these powers themselves come from
God, so that in using our abilities we are simply making use of
what God has already provided.

(2) Even if what we seek is not within our normal powers
of attainment, God will not necessarily provide for the situation
in the manner and in the terms which we desire. Remember that
St. Paul asked of God three times to remove the sting of the
flesh and the reply came "My grace is sufficient for you. Power
is made perfect in infirmity." But the point is that, even if God
did not provide for Paul by taking away the infirmity, He did
provide for him by giving him the grace to bear it to his ultimate
advantage.

(3) Where natural means are available, such as the help of
skilled physicians or the like, one cannot reasonably expect God
to work miracles to bring about a solution to the problem. As
one man said not long ago: "If two aspirin can take away a pain,
you can hardly expect God to intervene in a special way." The
same principle can be applied all the way down the line: if a
standard operation can save a man's life are we to be surprised
that a miracle is not forthcoming? If a satisfactory loan can be
arranged with the bank, should God supply money out of thin
air? If a suitor rejected by his beloved will shortly be able to find
a more attractive fiancée, should God be expected to step in and
preserve the first relationship? One cannot help observing, however, that in all these instances the solutions are in fact provided
by God. The skills of the trained surgeon come from God,

wealth comes from God, human beings come from God. God is present and providing at every moment in our lives. And if, as in the case of Paul, He does not provide the material means we seek, the spiritual means, which are ultimately more important, are always available.

Having laid down three negative principles, let us now consider three positive lines of thought. The overlapping with what has just been said will be obvious.

(1) God in fact provides for every situation as long as we trust in Him and do not commit deliberate sin. He provides for us in one way or another, although not necessarily in the way which we would here and now prefer. Here is an example from a priest's experience:

"For a while, as a result of a crippling accident, I found it very difficult to say Mass in church. Nevertheless as a pastor I had a strong desire to perform my liturgical function for my people. Yet I never knew from day to day whether I would be able to get through the Mass without collapsing on the altar. Naturally I prayed for God's help and, as a matter of fact, I never did collapse, although there were some days when I simply had to ask in advance for another priest to take my place. Yet whenever I did mount the altar there was always the possibility that I would not be able to complete the Mass and might have to be carried back to the rectory. I kept saying to myself 'God will provide.' Then I would add the phrase 'one way or another.' Either I would be able to complete the Mass or I would not. Whatever the case I knew that I would receive the grace to accept and respond to God's will and thus would be capable of pleasing Him although I myself might not be pleased with the immediate result.

"I knew too that the people would have the grace available to accept my infirmity in a spirit of Christian sympathy and understanding, even though they might be inconvenienced by my physical limitations. Therefore I told myself there was nothing to fear, for, whatever the circumstances, the will of God could be carried out. God could be pleased, in other words, and if God were pleased, who would have the right to be displeased? What was life all about except to please God and thus to live truly in a spirit of Sonship, with all the attendant sharing in divine life both here and hereafter? One way or another, the Lord provided."

(2) Through prayer and confidence we find strength, even of the natural order, which we didn't know we had. It is generally acknowledged by students of the question that human beings only actualize a small percentage of their potential in the physical and, most especially, in the mental and moral orders. By means of the strengthening of motivation and the stirring up of latent capabilities through prayer one can accomplish a great deal more than one anticipates, even in the most challenging circumstances. There are numerous testimonies in world literature, particularly in auto-biographies, which confirm the fact that persons who thought themselves incapable of one further step were able, by prayer for strength, to win the race, climb the mountain, row the boat, or overcome the mental and moral obstacles to a point which seemed far beyond their known capacity.

(3) In spite of all that has been said, it is nevertheless true that God seems to exercise a special providence and sometimes even a miraculous providence over those who abandon themselves to Him with a totality of trust and confidence. To prove this it is only necessary to read the spiritual literature of the Church, particularly the lives of the saints, and most especially the Bible itself. When Abraham was taking Isaac to be sacrificed to God, Isaac, not knowing that he was to be the victim, asked his father where they would find the victim, since there didn't seem to be any animals about. Abraham's reply is the seed of Judeo-Christian trust: "The Lord will provide, my son." And the Lord did provide a goat in place of Isaac, although such a substitution seemed extremely unlikely at the time. Thus God has intervened down through all the centuries, even to the latest saint who, having no food to feed the poor, prays with abandon to God, then turns to find the kitchen stocked with goods beyond belief. The Mother Theresas of the world will never be without God's special help. If we could only believe and trust as they believe and trust, we would not question the fact that "The Lord will provide."

19.

PRESENCE

A priest said recently: "When my mother died some years ago, Cardinal Spellman came to the wake. He could have sent flowers or a note or even ignored it entirely, for I was a young priest. I had done some special work for him, it is true, but certainly there was nothing about my relationship to him which placed any obligation on this busy prelate to go out of his way to be present on this occasion. But his presence meant a great deal to me and to my family at a time when it really counted, and none of us has ever ceased being grateful. When he came he said nothing memorable or striking, just the usual words of commiseration. He did lead us in a prayer, I remember, the 'Our Father,' I believe, and perhaps the 'Hail Mary' and the 'Gloria,' followed by the usual petition for repose for the departed. Though there was nothing inspiring in his words, his actual presence was eloquent and consoling in a way which could not be encompassed by words."

Everyone has had similar experiences, when someone's presence in a moment of trial or even a moment of joy has been far more expressive and strengthening than the banalities which were exchanged. One has only to reflect upon such experiences to realize that personal presence is one of the most significant and helpful gifts we can give to others.

The incarnation of Christ comes immediately to mind. "The Word was made flesh and dwelt among us." This need not have been so, theologians declare. God could have redeemed us, have saved us at a distance, as it were. He chose to send His only begotten Son to take to Himself a human nature like ours in everything but sin, to live among us, to heal us, to show us how to live and how to die and enable us to rise again. This appeals to all mankind so deeply and touchingly precisely because of the fact that His mercy involved His presence among us. We needed Him and He came to us.

We believe that He is still among us in many ways—in the Church, in the Eucharist, in the Sacraments, in His word, even in others. When two or three are gathered in prayer He is present. It isn't that He says anything new to us, anything that He hasn't said before, but He makes what He has said, and what He stands for, and what He is, a fresh gift to us at every encounter, strengthening, transforming, sanctifying. His words and actions take on meaning only from the reality of His personhood, the Divine Being Himself in our midst, even sharing our nature.

The presence of Christ is not merely a presence but a loving presence. That is part of the fullness of "being there." Individuals can be on hand in a room with us but not be present to us as a gift, that is to say, with loving concern. Some persons stand or sit in proximity to us but their attitude is that of the negative critic or, less offensively, the indifferent observer.

"Being there" means carrying out the words of the song, "Of My Hands I Give to You."

Even on the positive side there are various degrees of presence. A person can be there with a warm, giving inner feeling that permeates his manner and attitude even though he does not perform any particularly constructive actions, or utter any especially illuminating words. This is the first degree of presence and one which is very valuable in itself. But if the same person then proceeds to minister to the needs of the others, this is real gain. And, if in addition, he makes his presence available not only at this moment but at any moment of need, in a posture of creative assistance, then indeed his gift of presence is complete. This is what God does for us in Christ.

If a child met Jesus on the road, then ran home to tell his mother about it, what would be the first thing he would say? "Mother, I just met Jesus on the road." A description of what Jesus said and did would come later. The presence itself is the great gift from which all the others flow.

From reflections such as these we should come to realize that we must as Christians be more generous with the gift of presence which we possess. Many social gatherings and committee and organization meetings are almost incessantly boring and we have often wondered, no doubt, why we should make the sacrifice of attending them. In fact many of us must admit that we have often made excuses not to attend them. These excuses usually are related to the fact that we have few if any ideas to contribute, or we perceive little that we could personally gain from such encounters. But we cannot deny that our presence would have lent something positive if it had been a generous presence, not merely a carping one. We cannot define what this presence would have contributed, but it would have been at least supportive of others in their good purposes. It would have given them a sense of strengthening solidarity, of having one more in the fraternity of friendship or social action. Who can deny that the success of a gathering is often judged by the number present? Putting your body on the line has been the theme of effective social action in recent years.

The tendency of busy or shy or lazy persons is to reduce their presence to a minimum. Instead of visiting a person in his hospital room one can send him a card or even call him on the telephone. Instead of calling on the poor man in his hovel one finds it easier to send him a check. A Mass card will serve in place of attendance at the funeral, or a gift from Tiffany's will readily excuse one from participating in the wedding celebration. These things are a form of presence, it is true, but they fall short of the full Christian gift of self. There is really no substitute for "being there," when it counts. An object, a piece of writing, even a voice can never be the equivalent of a presence, that mysterious incommunicable center of existence, of spirit, of truth, of love.

Personal presence can be overdone, of course. We are all familiar with the "pest" who will not let others alone and who shows up at the most inopportune times. There is the case of a hospital chaplain whose over-conscientiousness led him to visit the patients too often in their rooms. But this is rare; most people seem to be too stingy rather than too extravagant with their gift of self.

The more one explores the question of significant presence the more one realizes how mysterious it is, how difficult to express in words. No doubt the fact that presence is existential, experiential, is the reason why mere words are inadequate. Yet the importance of presence can be grasped in many ways, perhaps most vividly by its opposite, namely absence. Consider the death of a loved one, particularly a parent or spouse, and you can gain some glimmering of the importance of personal presence. A much-loved mother dies, at an advanced age perhaps, and yet her passing leaves a gap which nothing, no one, can fill. Others can do what she did and say substantially the same things she said but no one can replace her as a person. Where the relationship has been close, part of the son or daughter seems to die when the mother dies.

Oddly enough, although personhood is defined as incommunicable, the highest degree of union can occur only between persons. Here the mystery grows too deep for utterance. But separation through death tells us something real and sublime about the importance of just "being there," with a loving heart.

20.

NOT TO IMPRESS BUT TO BLESS

The words of Christ: "I am come to minister, not to be ministered unto" are rich in possibilities for application to the Christian life. There are two principal emphases which stand out, namely service and humility. Would it be wrong to say that service and humility in gospel terms are almost, if not quite, interchangeable? The humble man is precisely the one who puts himself at the service of others. It is not simply a question of beating his breast and acknowledging his faults and refusing to take the first place at the table, although these elements are not absent. Christ Himself *washed* the feet of His disciples at the Last Supper. By His own testimony He was giving them an example of how they should serve others, an example which has always seemed a supreme act of humility.

One cannot help noticing that the example which Christ stressed was one of *dynamic* humility, that is to say an attitude or posture which leads to saving, helping, healing, loving others. In the pericope of St. Paul in Philippians, wonder is expressed at the humility of the Son of God Who "humbled Himself, taking the form of a servant." The emphasis on humility opening out to service cannot be ignored, particularly when the Epistle adds that He "became obedient unto death, even unto the death of the cross." It is not surprising that when the apostles were arguing among themselves as to who would be the greatest, Christ informed them that the greatest among them would be the servant of all the rest. "He that exalts himself shall be humbled, and he that humbles himself shall be exalted."

It is interesting that nowhere do we find Christ denigrating human gifts and instructing His followers that they must regard the talents bestowed upon them by God as of little value. He Himself tells them that they are "worth many sparrows" and that all the hairs of their heads are numbered. No doubt he demands a realism about their tendency to sinfulness, their total dependency on God, and the dangers of an inflated ego. Yet Christian humility is not treated as a mere intellectual or abstract self-devaluation, but as a posture of availability to the work of God and the needs of others, an unselfishness which blossoms out into loving and saving action. The authentically Christian attitude of humility, therefore, is not to seek praise for oneself but to make use of one's praiseworthy gifts to ameliorate the lot of others. To speak of the humble Christ or the humble Christian is to speak of a man for others. All this may perhaps be summed up in a suggested motto for followers of Christ: "Not to impress but to bless."

Unfortunately the egotist tends to distort the motto so that, although he does not eliminate service and in fact may even emphasize it, he makes it subordinate to the impression which he hopes to make. His re-phrasing might run: "Not so much to bless as to impress." Since such an attitude is rarely present in the conscious mind of a "concerned Christian," it may take years before he realizes that concern for self has really been at the root of his concern for others.

There are various clues, however, which can help him to discover the imbalance in his motivations and attitudes. Does he have a fear of failure which is unrelated to God or neighbor but which threatens his own self-esteem? In proclaiming the Christian attitude or position in public or private encounters, is he more concerned about receiving the plaudits and other marks of approval that may result than in communicating the message itself? After his presentation is over, do his thoughts run to the question "how did I do?" or "have my listeners really been helped to appreciate

Christian teaching more thoroughly?" Is he more concerned about making a hit than being the occasion of a genuine change of heart and mind? Does he find himself indulging in insincerities, distortions, dramatic discussions and tricks and gimmicks, or sincerely breaking the bread of the word of God? Does he see himself as an instrument and servant of grace and truth or does he really strive to be their master? Is he sufficiently aware of the fact that the riches of Christianity must be presented in a Christian way or else their authenticity is lost? In a word, is he serving himself or others?

Some active followers of Christ lament the fact that despite genuine efforts and sacrifices, they seem to have accomplished very little in the way of bringing forth Christian fruit. There can be many reasons for these "failures," but one reason which cannot be ignored is the fact that many times, perhaps more often than not, egotism can be detected readily by the average man. He may hear the words of Christ and even see the acts of Christ but he does not see Christ Himself, only Mr. X who has donned the Christian mask for his own exaltation.

"Not to impress but to bless." When such a motto is reflected upon and made part of one's thinking and attitudes, then a whole new tone and emphasis are given to even simple and unpretentious activities for the betterment of the other.

The tone is the genuine Christian tone, the tone of real loving concern and generously unselfish outreaching, which finds its fulfillment in the enhancement of the other.

The emphasis is on that which makes Christ more evident, which reveals Christ and His teachings and actions most effectively, for the sake of the other and not for the sake of oneself. "He must increase while I must decrease." Ways and means are chosen not because they will make a hit for the apostle, win him popularity and influence, but because they will least distort the realities to be communicated, rather enhancing them by placing them in the best possible setting.

Moreover, the motto "not to impress but to bless" brings a whole new sense of relaxation to the person who adopts it as his own. No longer does he have to worry about questions like "How did I do?" or "Will I be well received?" The desire to please gives way to the desire to help, to serve, to bless. Hence the personal insecurities of the apostle are no longer dominant because he realizes, in trying humbly to do Christ's work, he will achieve whatever effectiveness God intends him to achieve here and now. The surprising paradox is that in shifting the burden from himself to God and changing his motivation from himself to others, the yoke becomes sweet and the burden light. No one is so relaxed in his relationships to others as the really humble Christian. Yet this relaxation does not diminish but increases his loving concern and fervor.

This attitude, like its opposite, can readily be noticed by people of every type. In general they respond accordingly. They can tell the difference between Christ and his counterfeits. "He who humbles himself shall be exalted."

21.

CHRISTIAN MATURITY

Everyone has a different idea of what constitutes maturity, whether Christian maturity or otherwise. Some seem to link it primarily to age and experience, while others would acknowledge that a high degree of maturity can be attained by a knowledgeable young person who possesses what people call "an older head." Some would not allow anyone to be mature until at least middle age but would point out that this in itself is no guarantee. A person can have a mature body and a great deal of actual experience and yet be sadly lacking in the judgment and the balance which are deemed necessary for maturity. Some would point out the further fact that a person can be mature, so to speak, in matters concerned with his specialization in life, yet lack the broader experience and knowledge which are so important to authentic adulthood.

One need not enter into a debate on this subject or choose sides in order to see that certain elements are required by any reasonable view of maturity. These include a degree of knowledge, judgment, and experience and the ability to see life in terms of its authentic values. Moreover, one must see these values in perspective and form a sense of priorities which enables one to make appropriate decisions and choices, in other words to live out one's life in a way that is fully responsive to the reality of things.

When we speak of Christian maturity, we may include these

factors as permeated by the supernatural realities of revelation and grace.

Christian writers have generally described the mature follower of Christ as one who enjoys to a high degree the gifts of the Holy Spirit, that is to say the gifts of prudence, fortitude, knowledge, understanding, wisdom, piety and fear of the Lord. Maturity of this type is not merely the result of one's own efforts but is a gift of God made available in different degrees to different persons, usually in proportion to the response which a person makes to grace under grace. Because the gifts of the Holy Spirit are precisely gifts, it can happen that even a very young person and one relatively inexperienced in the ways of the world may yet have a high degree of maturity when it comes to understanding God's will and living out the Christian life. "God has chosen the weak things of the world to confound the strong, the foolish to confound the wise."

It is evident then that the wisdom of the Christian may often be foolishness to other people.

In that sense Christian maturity is not merely a baptizing of natural maturity; it has its own priorities and its own experiences which make it singular in human endowment.

But if knowledge and experience and prudence are necessary on the natural level, they are even more necessary on the supernatural, although their orientation may be quite different. The mature Christian must surely be one who knows not only the basic elements of the gospel but its richer implications in terms of his own milieu and in terms of whatever guidance he may be called upon to give others. One can't forget the opinion of the great Saint Theresa of Avila that she would prefer to have as her guide in Confession a knowledgeable priest rather than a very pious priest who was lacking in deep understanding of revelation and its appropriate application for his penitents. Most of us have met people who possess a high degree of holiness but who seem to have a certain narrowness in their interpretation of the Christian life. One could not view them as entirely mature Christians although they do possess a certain maturity of virtue, if not of judgment.

Experience, not so much in worldly terms, but primarily in the ways of God and in encountering the crises of the Christian life also seems to be part of the make-up of the authentically mature Christian. However, it is true that God can give insight even to those with very little personal experience of crises and their ramifications; this has no doubt happened in the case of many of the saints. This would involve extraordinary graces which one would accept thankfully from God but which one would not presume upon without some clear sign.

The gift of prudence is perhaps the most significant mark of the mature person. But in the case of the Christian it can well be a prudence that sometimes seems imprudent to others. There is a golden prudence and a yellow prudence, the yellow variety leading one to unChristian compromises and to avoiding ventures into new areas of service to Christ and one's fellow man. Golden prudence walks on the waters; yellow prudence will not even leave the boat.

What are some of the elements in this prudence? One factor of importance is to see "life steadily and see it whole," to use a cliché which is not without meaning in this context. It means to appraise realities as to their true value and to view reality in all its extent and multiplicity. To put it another way, this Christian realism is not ready to leave out certain elements of value in favor of a partial view which might permit of readier solutions. This implies a certain sense of perspective which does miss the whole for the parts or vice versa. It tends to view life's realities in their genuine relationships, having an instinct for the harmony of the universe while not neglecting individual values because of concern for the whole.

Such considerations lead to what might be the most decisive element: a divine sense of priorities. The mature Christian sees things as God sees them, inasmuch as this is possible. His decisions are made on the basis of the priorities in the gospel. "Seek ye first the kingdom of God and His justice and all these things shall be added unto you." Once again this sense of priorities may not correspond to worldly thinking. Often quite the contrary is true.

Mature Christians are often very impractical people by worldly standards. That is as it should be. In making any decisions for himself or in giving any guidance to others the mature Christian asks himself one primary question: "What is God's will in this matter?" On this level his sense of priorities is unassailable.

But very often it is difficult to determine God's will. Gospel teachings seem sometimes ambiguous or at least applicable in one case and not in another. The basic ten commandments are evident, but when it comes to the application of the commandment of love it is not always easy to determine the truly loving thing in this situation here and now. Nor is it by any means easy to determine in advance what course of action will create conditions most favorable to the glory of God. In such situations knowledge and experience are invaluable but the guidance of the Holy Spirit through his gifts is decisive. The truly mature Christian is the one who is most responsive to the movements of the Spirit, and the Spirit leads where He wills.

It would be too bad if these thoughts were to be interpreted as suggesting that prudent Christian judgment is all that we expect from a mature Christian. Such prudence is essential but the mature Christian is also a person of mature virtue across the whole spectrum of the Christian life, a virtue which has deepened and mellowed and grown as a result of profound contemplation of God's truth and responsiveness to God's grace. The mature Christian is many splendored, especially rich in faith and hope and, most of all, love. He or she is the one who makes realistic Paul's admonition: "Let this mind be in you which was in Christ Jesus," and his stirring cry: "For me, to live is Christ."

22.

THE STYLE OF CHRISTIANS

Christian doctrines and morals are one thing; Christian style is another. Style is of course related to the other two and should permeate, and be permeated by, them both. Unfortunately we all know many instances of moral Christians proclaiming the authentic gospel in a way which, upon examination, seems repulsive not only to other human beings but to God Himself. Let us consider a few examples.

A first example of Christian content with unChristian style is drawn from the pages of *Playboy* magazine, which, as everyone knows, is dedicated to nourishing sensuality in men. A certain religious order, seeking to serve God by increasing the number of priestly vocations saw fit, we are told, to publish an advertisement in this sex-saturated magazine. The advertisement was not marred by sensuality itself but the very context in which it appeared could not help but taint its message. One might not have argued if the advertisement had admonished the readers to reject their lustful attitudes and thus begin to move toward real Christian living, which might, in the long run, lead to vocations. But it partook of the quality of casting pearls before swine, offering leadership in the Christian life to those who had not yet even been converted from lust. The intention was good, the advertisement itself was Christian in content, but the setting, the ambience partook of Madison Avenue not of the Via Dolorosa.

A more classical example of Christian content without Christian style is the functioning of the Holy Office during certain periods in church history. The purpose of the Holy Office was evidently the preservation of the purity of faith and morals. In fact, however, at certain lamentable times, torture was used in the questioning of those suspected of heresy. Even until recently, long after torture had been eliminated, a person in some cases was not allowed to know fully the charges against him, much less to examine them and to reply to them point by point. All this has now been changed, we are told. That is all to the good, but a black mark has been laid upon the church's history which can never be eradicated. In their exaggerated zeal, even God's holy men have forgotten that there is a Christian way of doing things and that if certain worthy objectives cannot be attained except by a style of action out of harmony with the gospel, then the matter must be left in the hands of God.

In academic terms there is the case of the over-eager Board of Trustees of a religious college. Understanding the importance of Catholic education, the need to maintain a Christian voice on the college level and to promote Christian living among young people, the Board invests the college money in speculative ventures on the stock market. "After all," they tell themselves, "unless we increase our endowments the college may have to close in a relatively few years." Thus for the sake of Christian truth and morality, this high-minded group may engage in all the sordid tricks and security maneuverings which the capitalistic system permits. Whether they make money or not does not affect the principal point under consideration. By reason of a sort of spiritual myopia they have neglected the Christian style of life and substituted worldliness in the most perjorative sense as the instrument of accomplishing Christ's purposes.

In none of the above cases has anything illegal been done in terms of laws of the times. In fact, a sort of legalistic mentality has obviously colored all these actions to the point where we can have no doubt that they would be disowned by Christ Himself.

This legalism can also occur on the person-to-person level of

Christian living. The father who in his zeal for God's will exercises undue severity toward his children, harshly punishing every slightest infraction of his family mandates, the Catholic schoolteacher who insists that every jot and tittle of his assignments be perfectly carried out, the employer who considers it a service to God to require of his workers every ounce of their available energy—all these conscientious people, who no doubt consider themselves and are considered in their communities as outstanding Christians, in fact only succeed in stirring up rebelliousness against the very faith which they confess. They have done the "right thing" in the "wrong way," a way which, while it may not be strictly immoral, is strictly unChristian. In this sense, in the eyes of many, the style is the man and if the style is unChristian, the man is equally so.

The list of examples of Christian content with unChristian style can be extended at will. Certain emotional methods, the use of materialistic commercial means to "enhance" Christian institutions, the application of rules and regulations in a heartless, unfeeling manner are only some of the many ways in which Christ can be betrayed by the very persons who profess to serve Him. In a different context, Jesus prophesied that His true followers would be persecuted by those who thought they were doing a service to God.

It would seem important, therefore, to undertake either personal or communal Christian enterprises with deep positive concern about the Christian style in which they are to be carried out. Certain questions will certainly be apposite. For example, it should be asked: Are these acts or plans compassionate in their means as well as their aims? Does this enterprise breathe a spirit of worldly materialism or is it permeated with an authentic gospel tone? Does it give due weight not only to some Christian values but to Christian values in all phases and modalities? Is it an endeavor which gives rise to Christian renewal or does it simply reinforce and perpetuate pagan modes of procedure? Does this personal or institutional activity achieve its well-intentioned effect primarily through a form of human manipulation or coercion or does it respect genuine Christian freedom in all its dimensions? Is this apparently worthwhile procedure calculated to encourage low sensuality or other demeaning qualities, or is it rather permeated by an elevation of spirit, indeed even an austerity which breathes of the redeeming cross? Perhaps all these questions can be summarized in one: Is this the way the loving, self-sacrificing, freedom-conferring Jesus would have us do it, the same Jesus who renounced the worldly spirit in all its forms?

One looks back in puzzlement at certain phases in the Christian pilgrimage when slavery, torture, conquest, and the like were all too readily tolerated, and one realizes that God's holy people individually and even in large collective numbers can be so absorbed in Christian content that they all but lose a Christian sense of style. And the more one meditates upon this danger the more one sees that careful reflection on this subject is a constant need if Christ is not to be left out of Christianity. Perhaps the followers of Christ should pray every day that they should not only be orthodox in their beliefs, virtuous in their morals, but also Christ-like in their style of action.

23.

A WARM AND LOVING HEART

Perhaps you remember reading a story about a good priest who, although he said his prayers and performed his duties in a spirit of dedicated obedience to God's will, found that he was not as effective in his ministry as his virtuous conduct might have suggested. People did not seem to warm up to him; they took their problems and their spiritual needs to other priests, some of whom were less notable for their piety and strict fidelity to the rules of the spiritual life. The priest in question was careful to make his meditation every day, to prepare his sermons meticulously, and to display the appropriate attitudes toward the people—yet all to little avail. The flock did not seek him out, but in fact avoided him when possible.

What was the missing ingredient in the make-up of this apparently exemplary pastor? Only after long experience and reflection did he realize that he was marked by a clear deficiency which, although it had for a long time been unrealized by him, was obvious to all around him. The mark was the mark of lovelessness; he seemed to lack a warm and loving heart. People can forgive all sorts of short-comings in a Christian but this is one which they cannot tolerate. They will not be drawn to Christ by mere virtue unpermeated by recognizable lovingness. But of course this is all the more true if they are dealing with a priest, who is supposed to represent Christ in a very special way.

But to convict the priest of lovelessness was not entirely just either. He did love God and his fellowmen, as was clearly manifested by his service to both. Unfortunately, however, his love was almost entirely on the intellectual or abstract level. In his mind he valued and appreciated other persons and desired to bestow blessings upon them. But this love was really not manifested in his manner, in his way of relating to others. A sort of cool reserve based in part on natural temperament, in part on shyness, and in part on simple apathy, made him appear to others as lacking in sympathy and compassion. Hence the relative failure of his ministry.

No doubt there is a certain unfairness in the response (or rather the lack of response) of people in general to individuals such as the one just described. Temperament is often something "given," often not subject to extensive modification merely by will-power. A reserved person therefore simply has to work harder to radiate Christ to others. Usually it will take him much longer to be accepted, to exert the desired influence, but a constant plugging away, a constant stirring up of loving motivation cannot be ignored over a long period of time. The heart reveals itself at last. The dedication and concern must finally burn through the ice. The only danger is that the individual with the somewhat repellent personality will become discouraged at his failures and give up the effort to warm the flickering fires in his heart.

There are many reasons why he might become discouraged. Other individuals, not nearly so intelligent, perhaps not as talented, are able, without apparent effort, to wield wide influence for good. They seem to be gifted with a sort of common touch that enables people to communicate with them readily and enables them to communicate Christian values attractively. The shy, reserved person looks on in wonder as such an individual is greeted warmly on every side and sought out in moments of trial. The so-called "loveless one" cannot help wondering if the warm loving quality of the effective Christian is not really a mere natural gift of personality, not essentially related to Christ or the gospel. "Are not people being fooled," he asks himself, "by an unselfconscious, buoyant manner, while disregarding deeper qualities, deeper virtues?"

It would be hard to deny that in many cases people are fooled, at least for a time, by an attractive, affectionate manner which, in fact, may only be superficial in its implications. Whether such an attraction can endure over a long period involving stressful experiences is another matter entirely. But one would like to think that the dedicated Christian heart, whether it is lodged in the breast of a naturally outgoing, sympathetic person, or in that of a person with temperamental reserve, will in the long run make itself felt and succeed in drawing others to the heart of Christ.

No one, after all, can long succeed in ignoring the quality and motivations of someone who serves him with concern and dedication. The vision may be clouded; the observer may see through a glass darkly but eventually the view is clarified. In time even the frosty window transmits some light and heat.

What should the so-called loveless person do to eradicate the mark upon his brow? The first thing he needs is patience, endurance. He must come to realize that his effectiveness on a short-term basis will always be more limited than that of a warmer personality. But he must have confidence that by a persevering nourishment of union with the heart of Christ he will at last overcome the isolating barriers that make communion difficult. He must work harder to accomplish less than a more fortunate other. He must strengthen his motivation in prayerful meditation, trying to make present in himself not only the mind but also the heart of Christ Jesus.

Certainly he must not settle for the present frigidity of his temperament. He needs to stir up, by the warming grace of God, his sympathetic gift, whereby he can enter more realistically into the trials and problems, and even into the joys, of others. Although not everyone has an equal gift of sympathetic imagination everyone has some such powers, and they can be developed. Would it not be possible for a cool-hearted person to fan the flames by saying silently in his own mind when dealing with another person

"I love you in Christ and I love Christ in you."? This raising of consciousness, deliberately undertaken, has in fact been known to reveal itself in the tone of one's voice, the sympathetic quality of one's posture and gestures, and even in the light of one's eyes. Could not the mark of lovelessness be burned away by this constant stirring up of the heart through self-exhortation?

There can be little doubt that profound love of Christ, however unemotional in the beginning, creates its own emotional tone which carries over sooner or later to those who are loved in Christ. Reflection upon His teaching that whatever one does to His brethren he does to Him, and meditation on His commandment to love one another as He has loved us, if undertaken in a spirit of openness and real responsiveness, cannot fail to warm the heart and the atmosphere too.

But the loveless person needs a certain daring, a certain venturesomeness as well. He must be willing to appear ridiculous or at least awkward in his efforts to break out of the cocoon of reserve. For him, at first, it is a form of carrying the cross, and he must be prepared to stumble more than once. Experience will teach him to take one small step at a time in relating warmly to others; often only a little kindness is what is needed. But small steps soon carry one on farther than one thought one was capable of going.

For a Christian, because Christ abides in him, a warm and loving heart is always attainable, never to be despaired of.

24.

PRAYER AS SERVICE

One of the dangers of contemplative prayer is that it may become self-centered. This can happen in two ways.

The first way is through using God as a means of pleasurable satisfaction. When all goes well contemplative prayer can be delightful. There is a sense of peace, of the brightness of God's presence, of the healing and strengthening power of God's grace. Under such circumstances it involves what seems like a foretaste of heaven. True, such moments come more frequently for some persons than for others, but apparently there are a fair number of persons who habitually are blessed by this blissful form of prayer.

For them the problem arises: Am I praying because I truly love God and want to do His will more perfectly or am I primarily interested in the pleasurable satisfaction which I receive from contemplative union? Spiritual writers tell us that an individual can become greedy for this type of prayerful consolation. A warning is issued: we must seek the God of consolations rather than the consolations of God. But then one wonders why God gives consolations if He does not wish the recipient to enjoy them. Is not all pursuit of God in a way self-centered? Are we not taught to seek beatitude; does not our very nature, elevated by grace, reach out for the fullness of God's life and goodness, which are our total fulfillment?

These are difficult questions and ones which at times might

better not be asked because too much scrutinizing of contemplative prayer can complicate it to a point where it is marred or destroyed. Of course the individual seeks fulfillment in God; he cannot do otherwise, if he possesses the light and the good will. The real question is one of conscious motivation; is the individual entering into contemplative prayer primarily because it is God's will for him? Would he readily give up this form of prayer if he knew that it were contrary to God's will? Would he allow optional contemplation to interfere with clear and present duties in such a way that it could be said that he put his own prayerful pleasure above God's will? If that were true, then here would be a case of selfish prayer. Otherwise the matter had best be left to God's providential action. Consolations in prayer are not so easily come by that they should be rejected because of some scruple about self-indulgence.

Indeed they have many positive values apart from personal enjoyment. The delights of prayer lighten the whole burden and atmosphere of Christian life and by releasing personal pressure enable one to direct his energies to serve others. Prayerful delights may help the individual take on difficult, seemingly impossible tasks and may serve as a guiding light in the midst of troublesome, otherwise insoluble problems. These holy delights create an atmosphere of joy and peace in one's service to the Lord which is communicated to others in a salutary way. In this sense, such prayer can be a means of service not only to one's self but to others, to the greater glory of God.

A taste of heaven from time to time or even frequently should normally therefore be a great boon in building up the kingdom of God on earth. We must never forget that Jesus told His apostles to come apart with Him for a while: "Come to Me ye who labor and are burdened and I will refresh you." Having tasted heaven, how can anyone be willing to settle for anything less? How can sin have the same allurement which it once may have had?

No doubt there have historically been some strange cases of prayerful men and women who gave every impression of holiness in their private lives, so to speak, but failed to manifest this in their human relationships. This realization leads us to what some consider to be the second great danger of contemplative prayer: the temptation to withdraw from human relationships and to concentrate on one's isolated perfection.

Interestingly enough, the Catholic press recently reported that two priests had condemned so-called "transcendental meditation" on this very score. These critics maintained that it rendered its practitioners indifferent or at least apathetic with respect to the needs and problems of the society around them. It was alleged that the transcendental meditators in the pursuit of their private goals sought refuge from the distractions of humanity in a kind of hermit-like existence. One wonders if these priests were not at the same time making a veiled attack upon the contemplative orders of the Church.

Without entering into the merits of "transcendental meditation," we can affirm that the genuine Christian contemplative life can never be indifferent to the plight of the world. Apart from being a sign to the whole world of God's saving and transforming power, the Christian contemplative life seeks to call down that power on the world. Its orientation is supremely social in the sense that its followers offer themselves as an oblation for others.

In this sense it is possible to withdraw from the world in order to save the world.

For most Christians, however, the dictum of St. Thomas Aquinas is relevant: *"Contemplata tradere aliis."* Having absorbed the life and strength and presence of God, one enters into relationships with others in such a way as to communicate the divine gifts to them. If one fails to do this, then the nature of his contemplation is itself faulty. Contemplative prayer which does not lead to transmitting God in Christ to others must be inauthentic at the root. Either the individual is indulging in some kind of psychological daydreaming or self-adoration which he confuses with genuine contemplation, or, having enjoyed God's gift, he willfully refuses to respond to the demand for diffusion. *"Bonum diffusivum est."* Good is diffusive of itself. Is it conceivable that one could genuinely unite himself in prayer with Christ and not be concerned in a very real way with loving and serving others? How could it be that Jesus who said "A new commandment I give you that you love one another as I have loved you" would not demand this response from one to whom He had communicated Himself in the intimacy of contemplative prayer?

No, we can only say that either contemplative prayer was never truly present or, if it was present, the individual either deliberately or through some psychological disorder has failed to respond to its necessary implications.

Genuinely Christian prayer therefore is service. It implies that the individual himself is filled with God to the point of overflowing. This overflow is precisely God's gift through him to others. Desirably, however, the prayerful individual is not just a pipe through which God flows, as it were, to others. In that case he himself would retain little or nothing of God; his own soul would be relatively unchanged. One thinks of the old saying: "Be a cistern not a pipe." The cistern overflows but remains full in itself. A pipe retains nothing. Contemplative prayer will not long continue unless the person who is God's instrument is transformed in himself. Contemplative prayer is service to all: the contemplative and those around him.

25

WILLING FAITH, HOPE, LOVE

The Bible is very plain about the need to make acts of the will in regard to faith, hope and love. At the very end of St. Matthew's Gospel, Christ proclaims to His followers that those who believe will be saved and those who do not believe will be condemned. The psalms in the Old Testament repeatedly exhort the people to "hope in the Lord," and this exhortation is repeated in various forms many times in the New Testament as well. Likewise, Jesus speaks of the two great *commandments:* love of God and of neighbor, and, according to the gospel of St. John, He tells His followers: "A new *commandment* I give you that you love one another as I have loved you." All this is very direct, almost matter of fact. No distinctions are made as to whether individuals *feel* like believing or hoping or loving. These virtues are viewed as a matter of willing: a person by God's grace can will to believe, to hope, and to love, or not; he is responsible for his commitment or lack of it to these virtues.

Why raise the question at all, if it is so obvious in the Scriptures? The reason is that a certain confusion about this matter has been generated in common thinking, in the more technical analyses of psychologists, and even in some of the effusions of well-meaning spiritual writers.

With regard to the common thinking of many Christians, and even non-Christians, faith is something you either have or don't have and would seem to depend very little on the person himself. For example, it is not infrequent for a Catholic to say "I'm afraid I'm losing the faith" as though it were a matter over which he himself had little or no control. Yet one would think that, if Christ had made it a matter of salvation or non-salvation whether one accepts the faith, the element of willing choice would necessarily play the dominant role in this virtue. How can one be losing the faith if he wills to retain the faith? Usually what the statement really means is that the individual has difficulties either with doctrine or with the demands of morality and therefore his will to retain the faith is wavering. But, granted that faith is a gift which would not be possible without God's grace, not to mention His revelation, can it be assumed that this grace is unavailable to those who know the obligation of willing faith? We cannot doubt that God will make such grace available to those who are willing to pray more fervently and work more earnestly toward the preservation and increase of their faith. But the will to believe (on reasonable grounds) is essential to faith and its preservation, just as the will not to believe is the ultimate factor in the rejection of faith.

The same observations, with suitable qualifications, are relevant to the virtues of hope and love. The Christian who says he is "in despair" may have forgotten that he has an obligation to hope as a deliberate free choice (once again based on reasonable grounds). Despair is a sin and therefore it implies an act of the will, for there is no sin without free choice. "Hope in the Lord" we are commanded.

Similarly, in the matter of love, some people complain that they have no love in their hearts for God or neighbor. This may be specified in terms of marriage where an individual maintains that he has "fallen out of love" with his spouse. But Christ commands love. He cannot command the impossible. Therefore it must be possible to choose to love even though emotions are absent which would be helpful in this regard. Likewise, the grace of God must be available so that with the proper motivation, the possibility of love can never be absent, however unworthy its object may seem.

As long as a person has freedom he can will to love.

Such comments as the above are sometimes frowned upon by certain psychologists. They shake their heads at the notion of "willing" human feelings. They feel that someone's feelings should rise spontaneously out of the individual's authentic emotional responses. Therefore to will to believe, to hope, to love is possibly to alienate one's self from one's own true feelings and thus create various types of psychological conflicts, which may stimulate neurotic attitudes, etc.

The answer is that the Bible is not speaking of faith, hope and love as "feelings" or "emotions." It is speaking of them precisely in terms of willed attitudes and commitments. The Bible is directing itself to the intellect and will of human beings, the psychologists primarily to the emotional and feeling level. Certainly it is not the intention of the Scriptures to eliminate or negate authentic emotion. Normally it can be assumed that, when the intellect and imagination present the proper motivations for faith, hope and love, the emotional level of man will respond positively. God is not asking men to believe in the unbelievable, to hope in the untrustworthy, or to love that which is not good. As a rule, therefore, when proper clarifications have been made, human feelings can be caught up harmoniously in the commitment of the virtues under consideration.

No doubt from time to time other factors will enter in (particularly in the case of neurotics) which will blind the emotions and feelings to the genuine values of faith, hope and charity and thus lead to conflicts. But obviously this would not call for the abandonment of these highest commitments; it would call for a working through of the conflicts so that the emotions can be adjusted to harmonize with and support what the individual knows in his mind and will to be right and true and good. But unfortunately some psychologists do not admit the existence of spiritual values towards which the whole of man, including his feelings, must be directed. This represents the psychologists' own problems in adjusting to the real order of values.

An occasional spiritual writer, in his well-intentioned effort to emphasize that salvation and therefore all supernatural virtues come from God and not from man, will tend to minimize the action of individual free will in accepting, maintaining and developing faith, hope and love. We may ask them, why does God command willing acts of faith, hope and love if man isn't capable of making such acts? The answer of course is that free will continues to operate under grace. It is true that no one could make saving acts of faith, hope and love without God's gift of grace, but, where a command is present, it may be assumed that this gift is always present and potentially operative. Therefore man must freely choose even though the power to choose freely in a saving way may be possible only by grace. This is not Pelagianism or semi-Pelagianism; it is a simple recognition of the fact that grace respects divinely created human nature and works through it according to its modalities.

One might be able to summarize these facts briefly as follows: no choice (for adults) equals no faith, hope or charity. No grace equals no saving choice. The difficulty with some spiritual writers is that they have placed such emphasis on the second proposition that they have tended to lead some unsophisticated souls to de-emphasizing the first.

Actually the biblical doctrine is a most consoling one. It means that the changeability of human emotions, so dependent as they are on the stimuli of changing circumstances, does not destroy or even mitigate the authenticity of the theological virtues. A man can be troubled by terrible difficulties regarding faith, almost overwhelmed by skeptical emotions, and still will to believe virtuously. He can be saddened by all sorts of difficulties which may stimulate feelings of abandonment and despair, yet will to hope and trust without offense. He can discover all sorts of unlovable qualities in his neighbor and feel emotions of repugnance, yet will to love. God's grace is with him, salutary motives are continuously present and clearly stated by Christ and the church, prayer is always possible. God looks for good will and good will is always possible under grace.

26.

NOT LOVING ENOUGH

Anyone who reads the Bible knows that sin and the remission of sin are large elements. This is true in the Old as well as in the New Testament. The prophets denounce the sins of Israel plainly and constantly and the psalms speak again and again of the need for God's mercy and for conversion on the part of His people.

It was no accident that Jesus was crucified between two thieves. He was used to such company and, in fact, in a sense preferred it. He had said to the critical scribes and Pharisees: "I am come to call not the righteous but sinners." He apparently often went to dinner with publicans and other sinners and for this He was roundly criticized by his enemies. He shocked the critics by telling them: "The publicans and harlots shall go into the kingdom of God before you." In another place He said: "There is more joy in heaven over one sinner who does penance than over ninety-nine just who do not need penance." It was typical of Jesus that, when the thief on the right turned to Him beseechingly, He should reply: "This day you will be with Me in paradise."

He fulfilled the prophecy in Isaiah as repeated in Mark: "And with the wicked He was reputed." He must have been right at home between two thieves because all His public life He had been driving devils out of those possessed and healing, reconciling, strengthening sinners. "Thy sins are forgiven thee; go and sin no more." These words seem constantly to have been on His lips. The woman taken in adultery is one example. At the last supper He offered His bloody death under the unbloody signs of bread and wine: "This is My body which is given for you. This is the cup of My blood which is shed for you and for many unto the remission of sins." When He appeared to the assembled apostles after His resurrection "He breathed on them and said: 'Receive you the Holy Spirit, whose sins you shall forgive they are forgiven them, whose sins you shall retain they are retained.' " We call Him our Redeemer, our Saviour, because He offered Himself to the Father for the remission of our sins. Catholics believe that He has communicated this power of remitting sins to His church through baptism and through the sacrament of reconciliation or penance. He shed His blood "for the life of the world."

All this is indeed most obvious to the least informed of Christians. Even if such a one did not know the Bible, he would only have to assist at the Catholic Mass to be constantly reminded of the need for repentance and the possibility of forgiveness. From the opening act of repentance there is the constant theme of beseeching God's mercy in Christ for the forgiveness of sin. The words of consecration, already noted, renew this theme and indeed make Christ's redemptive power present. The prayers before communion, including the Lord's Prayer, are a re-echoing cry for liberation from that which separates us from God and makes us unworthy sons and daughters. "Forgive us our trespasses as we forgive those who trespass against us." "Deliver us, O Lord, from every evil." "Lamb of God, You take away the sins of the world; have mercy on us." "Look not upon our sins but upon the faith of Your church." The repetition is endless. The emphasis is inescapable.

But who needs it? In our time very few seem to be willing to admit that they are sinners. True, there seems to be a great deal of evil in the world, if we are to judge by the newspapers and by our own observation. But there seems to be no deliberate fault, which is the essence of sin. Terrible evils but no one to blame! Everyone can exculpate himself either by reason of psychological or environmental pressures. The parents are blamed for the sins of their children and yet the parents profess innocence of any wrongdoing. One might be led to wonder why Christ had to endure such a bloody death for sinners when no one but saints will admit to sinfulness.

In Christian terms, of course, there is another side to the coin. Through baptism we believe that we were given a new sinless life that is nourished by prayer and the sacraments and by loving service to God and others. We believe that if mortal sins are committed after baptism, they can be washed away in the blood of the Lamb through contrition, especially in the sacrament of reconciliation. The Christian life is viewed as primarily a life of grace not of sin. Sin, at least in any grave sense, would supposedly be a rarity, an exception among authentic followers of Christ. Through the resurrected Christ Who has endured the crucifixion, Christians, it is believed, rise to new life, beginning in this world and continuing into eternity. The proper emphasis, it would seem, is the Easter emphasis, the emphasis on life, on a more abundant life in Christ—a positive, creative emphasis, not directed towards sin-chasing primarily, but toward growth in the Spirit, toward nourishing and building up the kingdom of God.

All this is true and yet there are problems. There is still the liturgy to remind us of our sinfulness and still the breast-beatings of the saints, many of whom considered themselves great sinners, potentially if not actually.

"Potentially if not actually,"—perhaps this is the key to the emphasis on sin even in the worship of devout Christians. It is an admission that one has been saved not just from the sins that one has actually committed but from the sins which one might have committed, had it not been for the prevenient grace of God, won for us through Christ. In a sense each one of us has been saved a thousand times from sins he might have committed except for God's healing strength in moments of temptation. How is it possible to live the good Christian life without the saving power of God? Lust is so simple, theft, lying, cheating, hating, hurting. These things come easily, require little effort. But to avoid them, to reject them, to turn away from them in a spirit of Christian faith and hope and love—this is a miracle of grace worked again and again, a redemptive gift won for us through Christ our Lord.

This is true of the past and equally true of the present and future. We can look on the public, unconcealed sinner and say thankfully but not with smugness: "There but for the grace of God go I." Redemption is an ongoing process not merely curative but preventive. We pray to be freed from our sinfulness not just in terms of the sins we have committed but in terms of the sins which we will avoid through His providential power.

But even so, even with all this healing and saving and preventive grace, who among us can say that he is without sin, at least in terms of venial faults? Anger, sloth, envy, greed, and the rest all make their mark in our lives, even though we may feel that we are constantly struggling against them. Perhaps our sin is not so much that we thoughtlessly succumb to these things from time to time, but that we fail to take the measures needed to root out these faults or at least to bring them under control. We fail to use psychological methods as well as those purely spiritual. We fail to examine our lives closely and to take prudent, mature measures to harness our evil tendencies. About other things we are prudent, studious, adult. In the matter of our habitual faults, however, some of us are all too careless in avoiding occasions of sin, in checking on their causes, in strengthening motivation, in permeating the small as well as the large aspects of our lives with God's presence and power. An act of contrition with a vague purpose of amendment may be all the care that we devote to eradicating weaknesses which, although not mortal, may be very painful to others.

Positively, we do not love enough and must learn to love more. This is a sovereign remedy for sin which, when prayerfully besought, will open our minds and hearts superabundantly to God's healing, perfecting, strengthening, life-giving Spirit.

27.

WHAT ELSE WOULD YOU BE DOING?

A young priest complained to his pastor about the work load in the large city parish. The pastor was constantly assigning him to special confessional periods at midday and in the late afternoon, to the distribution of communion at several masses a day, as well as to the preaching of sermonettes several times a week. All this was in addition to the young priest's regular days on duty.

"It's too much," the young priest told the pastor. "You're really pouring it on too heavily."

The pastor paused for a moment and then asked with a wintry smile: "What else would you be doing, Father?"

The young priest was indignant and turned away without answering. But, as he thought the matter over, he realized that the pastor had raised a valid question and one which revealed a large area of possible self-indulgence. Actually, he realized, if he had not been performing the pastor's assignments he would probably have been sitting in his room, idly paging through some magazine or novel, or staring at some vapid program on television, or just smoking and daydreaming. Possibly he could have been doing something else truly worthwhile, but there were many other hours in the day when such vital interests could be satisfied. "What else would you be doing?" Or the question might have been phrased more pointedly: "What else would you be doing that would be more important?" Indeed, compared with what he would be doing otherwise, the young priest's assigned tasks, directed wholly to the sanctification of fellow human beings, were sublime.

Whether priest, religious, or lay person—all need to reflect on the implications of this anecdote. Every Christian upon self-examination will discover that he resists actualizing his full potential for growth and service in the Christian life. Many have unconsciously set up a boundary beyond which they will not move: thus far and no farther. Viewing most phases of gospel living as a burden or at least an invasion into their "free" time and energy, they carry with them a faintly resentful aura as they plod away at those unavoidable tasks which their religious commitment "forces" upon them. Perhaps, if they were to ask themselves what else they would otherwise be doing that was more important, they might be brought up short to realize not only how much they have undervalued the work of the Lord, but also how stingy they have actually been in the disposition of their mental and physical resources.

There is the individual who resents even the "burden" of Sunday Mass. Certainly, with the schedules of today, Sunday worship cannot be blamed for cutting into a person's needed sleep. Is it possible that an hour's time on the Lord's day once a week can be a task of such magnitude that millions of people fail to attend Mass and others go with reluctance? What else would they be doing except idling about the house or the grounds? But in the balance of their self-centeredness, this minimal self-oblation in fraternity with their Christian brothers seems an enormous waste.

Many people pray with deep reluctance. To say a routine and distracted prayer or two, morning and evening, is about all they seem to be able to manage. If one suggested to them ten or fifteen minutes of meditative reflection on the Gospels twice a day they would throw up their hands in horror. And yet this practice might change the depth, the quality and the meaning of their lives. And what else would they be doing in these brief periods? Engaging no doubt in trifling and superficial actions which, although not totally without value, probably could not be compared with the substantial worth of loving prayerfulness.

On the other hand, even persons who do engage in regular

meditation often look forward to it with anxiety and even distaste, and then spend the time in fruitless distractions, which, although not fully deliberate, are the result of an unconscious aversion to the use of their time and energy in this fashion. Often they cannot wait until the allotted period of time for prayer is over. They think of everything else but God and, although at the end they have vague regrets for wasting the time, they do little to pave the way for deeper union next time. They need to discover the root of their difficulty and to examine this resistance to meditation and prayer. The unexamined life is often a life of waste.

Action groups and organizations are an abomination to many people. They recognize the legitimacy and need for such structures but they constantly find excuses for their own non-participation. Too often they tell themselves as well as others that they are "too busy," although, if they examined themselves, they would discover that they waste many unsatisfying and frustrating hours of leisure in sheer idleness or unproductive pursuits. Is there really anyone who is so authentically busy that he can't spare a couple of hours a month (or even a week) for organized efforts to improve the common good or to help to build up the kingdom of God?

What one sees here is not a real objective barrier but a mental block. For selfish (often unconsciously so) reasons the person has convinced himself that he has no time or no energy to spare. But what else would he be doing? When he might enrich his own life and the lives of others to the glory of God he is puttering around pointlessly in such a way as only to add to his fatigue and his sense of oppression by life. Though in the beginning he might have to force himself to act, he would soon find through the joyful experience of working with others in service that his life had actually been lacking in important dimensions. Fatigue and disappointment can disappear in the soul that is open to the onrush of the serving Spirit.

True, many are not available for regular organizational activities, but everyone is called to one-to-one charitable actions. How often do even good Christians resist this call! It seems such a burden to visit a sick person in the hospital, to attend a wake, or funeral, to console some lonely or depressed individual, to exercise hospitality to those who would benefit from it. And yet, upon analysis, what is so tremendous about the expense of time or energy in such loving acts? What else would the person be doing other than expending or pampering himself in various unproductive ways? With seven hundred and twenty hours in the month it is hard to see how the expenditure of an hour or two for the consolation of others in need can be such an extravagance, such an overwhelming task. The problem is not really the time involved or the energies expended but the unhealthy attitude which has developed unchecked. The failure to put one's motivations in order and, under grace, to stir up a lively, full-bodied appreciation of genuine values in life is a far greater obstacle to the living out of Christian charity than the actual expenditure of time and effort.

Some of these well-meaning Christians are (consciously or unconsciously) skeptical of Jesus' words: "My yoke is sweet and my burden light." They do not find it so. They accept the teaching on faith, perhaps, but it finds no resonance in their emotional convictions. Part of their problem is first, that they have not opened themselves fully to the healing and strengthening power of Christ in them, and secondly, they have not asked themselves the question: "What else would I be doing?"

28

VALIDATING FAITH

A current phenomenon is the desire to experience the realities of faith. God-experience is a key theme not only among Christians but even among devotees of Oriental mysticism. To some Christians who have had the notion that faith is precisely an act of commitment in the absence of experimental knowledge, this tendency seems to be an aberration and indeed a contradiction in terms. Did not St. Paul say that faith is the evidence of things that appear not? Where seeing takes place there is no more believing. Cannot one say the same about experiencing?

Interestingly enough, St. Paul also says that "the Spirit testifies to our spirit that we are the sons of God." And he sees no contradiction to the immateriality of faith in the charismatic experiences of the Corinthians. And what of Pentecost? The apostles experienced the coming of the Holy Spirit in flames and then experienced their power to communicate the Gospel to others in the streets of Jerusalem. And their auditors, hearing the apostles speak redemptive words according to the understanding of each listener, were also beneficiaries of a sort of supernatural experience.

One could go on listing from the Gospels and from the history of the saints innumerable examples of the experiencing of divine power in connection with the proclamation and the acting out of the Christian faith. Indeed most prayerful people, some more frequently than others, experience moments of union with God which go beyond the normal levels of intellect and will, whereby God seems to have touched their souls directly.

The experiencing of the realities of faith in a sort of validating way can also be expressed in other terms. When a non-Catholic, for example, becomes a Catholic and begins to live the spiritual and sacramental life of the Church and to follow its precepts of charitable service, he comes to appreciate, through experience, the teachings which he had already accepted intellectually and voluntarily upon his conversion. He realizes now, more than he ever thought conceivable, the authenticity of such doctrines as the in-dwelling of the Holy Spirit, the value of Christian love and humility and purity, the joy of prayer, the strengthening power of the sacraments, the peace of an absolved conscience. Experience gives a new dimension to his faith and serves to strengthen the commitment which he has already made.

It is, in a way, like an engaged person who has studied all about marriage and given assent to the traditional teachings and guidelines with respect to the marriage state. It is only after he has entered into marriage with a loving partner that he experiences the truth of what he previously acknowledged as true. The living out of the marriage relationship by persons of good will is, in other words, a sort of experimental validation of all that they have been taught. This, of course, is only an analogy, but it has some relevance even in the area of a supernatural religious commitment.

All of these reflections call us back to the apparently negative position based on the words of St. Paul: "Faith is the substance of things to be hoped for, the evidence of things that appear not." This would seem to suggest that if one experiences or *knows* a reality of faith, then faith is no longer present because it is no longer needed.

The problem is probably one of semantics or at least of the need to make distinctions. The Scriptures tell us that "no man has ever seen God" and yet every man, at least in the natural order, has seen in himself the effects of God's action. How could we know that God existed if we did not experience His creation? Some such application may be made to the supernatural order of the Christian life. A person may experience "touches" of God; may experience the power and effectiveness of God's grace both inwardly and outwardly; may experience the joy and peace which flow from the acceptance of the reality of faith without the full and direct vision which is normally reserved to the beatific life of eternity.

Once again an example may serve to clarify. A child *believes* that his mother is in the next room and this gives him a sense of joy and peace. He does not see his mother, although he has reason to believe that she is there. His faith in her presence gives him a sense of security and even of strength to put aside the fears of the night. He is, in a sense, having a faith experience. In his imagination he may even talk to his mother and find happiness in reflecting upon her anticipated response.

Like all analogies this one limps, perhaps more severely than most. This is true because God is not in the other room, but in our souls. His presence and power are not imaginary, but real. His teachings are not traditional common sense but often Divine mysteries which can only be understood, in their fullness, in the beatific vision, if then. The life of grace is truly supernatural and not a mere stimulation of latent human powers.

Perhaps it would be better to say that faith experiences are not the direct experiencing of the articles of faith themselves, but the experiencing of the effects which flow from commitment to these realities. In receiving the Holy Eucharist, one does not directly experience in all its fullness the real presence of Christ but one does experience the effect of this Presence in terms of loving peace and strength. Faith experience is, in a sense, the resonance within the believer caused by the faith realities. If one did not have faith these resonances would not occur. On the other hand, these resonances do not constitute faith.

In all honesty it must be said that for some persons these resonances do not occur, at least with much frequency. There are souls who must spend a lifetime in the dark night of an obscure faith which seems like a small and distant glow at the far end of a long tunnel.

For such persons, bereft of the strengthening consolations of validating experience, the words of Cardinal Newman are ever relevant: "Lead kindly light amid the encircling gloom; the night is dark and I am far from home."

There is a warning here too for *all* livers of the Christian life: the loss of faith experiences need not mean the loss of faith itself. Consolations, validating experiences can come and go; authentic faith, because it is a willed commitment under God, can and should endure to the end.

But, thanks be to God, most sincere followers of Christ enjoy validating experiences throughout their lives. This should not be a matter of surprise, much less one of anxiety. Many times in the Gospel Christ promises His followers that He will be "with" them. He promises to be "in" them. His "strength" is offered to them. He sends His Spirit upon them and He and His Father offer to come and make their abode in those who love Him and keep His commandments. He instructs Christians to eat His flesh and drink His blood under the signs or appearances of bread and wine. It would be strange indeed if the Christian in opening himself to such realities in a spirit of faith were not to experience in some way their impact in his being and in his life activity.

29.

STIRRING UP GRACE

Are you puzzled by the fact that the frequent reception of Holy Communion doesn't seem to make you very much holier than you were before? If you are married, do you wonder at the absence of spiritual growth in your relationship with your partner, even though the sacrament of marriage seemed to promise great things? What of confirmation and even of baptism? Why was it that in the case of the former you didn't suddenly become a strong and perfect Christian in any measurable, obvious terms? Does frequent confession leave you with your faults still in place, their force little diminished? If you have been blessed with the sacrament of holy orders, why is it that you sometimes look back on your first days in the priesthood as those of greatest holiness, greatest Christlikeness?

Several thoughts emerge from considerations of this type. First there probably is growth that you are unaware of. It may have been over a long period of time, not dramatic but very gradual, involving slow purification of motive with the almost unnoticeable (at any given moment) improvement in the quality of your spirituality. There may have been the step by step building up of your spiritual strength and reserve, which reveal themselves now in a stability of commitment which, although difficult to measure, gives you a greater sense of security in faith and virtue than would have been possible in the past. Just as a growing child does not experience his growth from day to day, yet is unquestionably involved in the process of growth, so too with the Christian life. The fact that the physically mature person may not enjoy the same sense of physical well-being as the child is obviously no negation of the maturing process which has taken place. Taken as a whole, there has been growth; there is greater strength, although the trials and even the disabilities may be proportionately greater as well.

A second consideration is related to the fact that a great deal of spiritual energy is needed simply to survive from day to day, even apart from any growth or strengthening. The analogy of the Eucharist to ordinary food is relevant here. On the purely physical level a person needs his daily food to maintain his energy and to ward off destructive illnesses. The taking of daily nourishment does not improve his health noticeably from day to day; it merely keeps him in a condition which allows him to function as well as he did yesterday. It would be an absurdity for him to say after his three meals: "How surprising that I don't feel any stronger today than I did yesterday at this same time! After all, I've had three more meals." Such an odd statement would, of course, miss the point of nourishment in an adult person. Its purpose is primarily maintenance, not improvement, except under certain specialized circumstances. In the case of the daily spiritual bread of the Eucharist the fact that one is enabled to maintain his spiritual level from day to day despite depleting forces, is in itself a great benefit. However, this comparison can be pushed too far. Each new reception of the Eucharist does indeed bring fresh graces which make the individual more holy and pleasing to God, even though he himself is not conscious in an experimental way of this effect.

The sacrament of penance or reconciliation can be analyzed along similar lines. It is, after all, a healing sacrament, restoring one to one's previous healthy condition spiritually. In the physical order when one is healed from an illness one does not expect to be stronger than ever: rather to regain one's normal good health. It is true, of course, that there are certain medications which build up strength and energy to resist diseases in the future. Here, too, there is an analogy with the sacrament of penance. Traditionally the Church has urged its frequent reception as an anecdote to sin and as a means of strengthening virtue. But in the case of mortal sins, these salutary effects are much more evident than in the matter of lighter faults. With regard to the latter one sometimes wonders why anger, impatience, selfishness, and the like are not totally banished by frequent confession. One is tempted to ask: "Is the sacrament at fault or the recipient?"

This leads to a further consideration, namely that because God in Christ operates through the administration of the sacraments (ex opere operato) the recipient, without any further effort on his part, may expect to be conscious of substantial spiritual benefit. Because of a certain type of training, a mechanical notion of the sacraments can easily develop. This type of thinking is frequently caricatured in terms of a vending machine: one puts in the coins and out comes the merchandise automatically. One receives the Eucharist and the outcome should be evident spiritual growth. Actually the vending machine analogy is not as absurd as it seems, for even there, although the merchandise emerges, it has little meaning unless made use of by the recipient. In the sacramental encounter it is true that God communicates graces to a believing, petitioning, open human being, but, as in the case of the material merchandise, the sacramental process will be of little apparent benefit unless the graces communicated are consciously "made use" of.

Here then is the crux. The words of St. Paul to Timothy are relevant: "I admonish thee, that thou stir up the grace of God which is in thee by the imposition of my hands." Timothy, it seems, had been ordained a bishop by Paul.

What can this mean, this stirring up of the grace of God? It would seem to mean exactly what it says. God communicates His Spirit in the sacraments as in other ways, but He expects His grace to be "used" in truly human fashion, that is to say, consciously, awarely, with full freedom. Christians are not puppets to be manipulated by the Spirit. The Spirit is in them and works in and according to their nature, which is intelligent, free. Graces are available but they must be valued and must be applied. A battery may store great power but this is wasted unless an intelligent being applies it to some need for energy. If he does not know that the battery exists or, knowing that it exists, is unaware that it contains power or, knowing that it contains power, does not use it, then its possible effectiveness is lost.

"Stir up the grace of God." If married couples were aware of the power given to them by the sacrament, the continuing power which does not cease on the day of their marriage, then they could consciously find great strength to overcome their trials and to grow in loving, spiritual union. The same is true of the priest or the confirmee. And if, when tempted or finding himself static in virtue, the individual were literally to stir up the graces of his confessions, wonders of spiritual accomplishment might take place. And would it not be possible too to go from strength to strength through frequent Eucharists, if a heightened awareness of God's renewed power were cultivated?

The problem then is a raising of consciousness together with a promotion of confidence. How? By the usual means given man to perceive more deeply and to act with stronger motivation. The usual means include meditation, contemplation, and a determined effort to walk in union with the Spirit Who is the Source of grace.

30

THE PROCESS

Much has been written about process philosophy and process theology, often to the great confusion of the reader. Some writers have even spoken about a process in God, which on the face of it seems repugnant to the established conception of God as ultimately perfect, without change or alteration. Not that authentic Christian theology regards God as static; quite the contrary. God is pure act. But this is quite a different thing from saying that God is in the process of becoming something which He wasn't before. Such an idea seems to be a contradiction of the very nature of God.

However, whatever criticism might be leveled against the proponents of process thinking (or at least against some of them), they have emphasized certain points which greatly needed stress in our day. They have forced Christians to focus their minds on the fact that all life, and especially Christian life, is a process of growth (or sometimes deterioration) and can never consist merely in the preservation of the status quo. Is this a new thought? Hardly, but it is one which needed revival to blast Christians out of their fortress mentality, which developed after the Reformation. This fortress type of thinking tended to stress preserving the state of grace, keeping the faith, avoiding involvement in situations which might prove dangerous morally and, in general, keeping one's self in a sort of spiritual cellophane wrapper which, although it prevented one from getting muddied, also prevented him from growing to his full potentialities.

It is not the intent of the present pages to analyze in detail the various limitations imposed by static thinking. But, as a simple example, one can think of how it might place a barrier to spiritual development in terms of the sacraments of confirmation and matrimony. If confirmation is considered over and done on the day the person is confirmed, with only a defensive posture to follow upon it, then a large measure of the meaning of the sacrament is lost. Confirmation should obviously be a permanent source of power and growth in the Christian life. Its graces are obviously intended to be stirred up and made freshly available for fresh efforts at witnessing and for new forward strides in Christian virtue.

In matrimony, too, if the couple were to consider their marriage sacrament to be total and complete in its implications on the day of their wedding, then how would their spiritual needs be specially catered to as the give and take of married life proceeded? Marriage like confirmation, and indeed like all the sacraments, is a sacrament of growth, particularly since like confirmation it is directed to a continuing relationship. It must, therefore, offer possibilities for growth or else it cannot serve the purpose for which it was established. This seems obvious enough, yet apparently many Catholics, and Christians generally, look back to their wedding day as the time when they received the sacrament of marriage, with no real sense of the applicability of the sacramental gift to the present problem or situation.

On a wider scale, one can think of first communion sermons which urge the children always to keep themselves as holy and innocent as on this blessed day. Not that such advice is wrong or unbiblical. St. James called upon Christians to keep themselves "unspotted from this world." But such a thought, it would seem, should always be balanced with St. Paul's admission of the fact that we cannot remove ourselves from this world and must work out our salvation within it. Such a balance must be adequately struck, without placing undue emphasis on self-protection rather than service to and involvement in the needs of others. Generations of children may have grown up thinking that the maintenance of the status quo in the spiritual life was the first and greatest commandment and perhaps the only one. As everyone knows, the two great commandments are love of God and of neighbor. Both of them demand a reaching out, a putting of one's self at the service of others, a forward movement toward new possibilities.

Jesus, in more than one of His parables, stressed the importance of a process of growth. Indeed He made clear that the failure to grow, to move forward, to expand in terms of one's Christian life will make one subject to condemnation.

The parable of the talents is an example of the importance of process. As recorded in the 25th Chapter of St. Matthew's Gospel, the master, upon going away, gave five talents, two talents, and one talent to three servants, to be used according to their ability. The first two servants put their talents to good use and doubled them by the time of their master's return. The third, being fearful of losing the talent and thus incurring his master's displeasure, buried it and had only this and nothing more to offer the master at the moment of accounting. Because of his over-cautiousness, his over-dedication to the status quo, his refusal to seek growth, the unprofitable servant had his talent taken away from him and was himself cast into exterior darkness. The importance of process in Christian terms could not be clearer than in this teaching of Christ Himself.

The parable of the mustard seed which grows into a tall tree or bush is also relevant in its own way. The Christian life is not a static affair precisely because it is a life and not a mere ethical system, a mere conformity to the dead letter of abstract laws. If the seed falling into the ground does not die it remains alone but if it dies then it will bring forth much fruit. "By their fruits you shall know them." Fruitfulness is a recurrent theme in the gospel, and the analogy which Christ draws between Himself as the vine and us as the branches, drives home this point with unambiguous force. "Every one that bears fruit He will purge that it may bring forth more fruit." God is not satisfied with the status quo; this is especially so because He gives us the means, His own Holy Spirit, to enter into spiritual process.

A study of the texts, indeed of the experiential data of the Christian life as it has been lived for two thousand years, reveals many elements in this life-long process. The first element is, of course, life itself. The nature of life on earth is vitality, movement, expansion, enrichment. When these qualities are absent, then death has either occurred or is setting in. One may wonder, therefore, how much authentic Christian life is present in the person who hugs his faith to himself and directs all his efforts merely to the preservation of the state of grace. Can grace be preserved in such a context, especially when Christ has proclaimed as His "new commandment" that "you love one another as I have loved you"?

A second facet of process is venturesomeness, which need not be the same as imprudence. It means a readiness to strike out in new directions, to seek out possibilities for service, and even to take risks for the purpose of building up the kingdom of God. Taking risks does not mean entering into possible occasions of sin but it does mean reinforcing one's self and strengthening one's self by the Spirit to enter into difficult situations where there is a possibility of significant gains for Christ. It means not being put off by every obstacle or being dominated by fears of one's own weakness, without taking into account the strengthening gift of God's Spirit. Christ Himself took innumerable risks. He risked His life many times, and at last was crucified. His life, death and resurrection are a judgment on those who would hide their Christian talents in a napkin and thus have nothing to offer by way of increase to their returning master.

Finally, because of human limitations, process will naturally involve a certain amount of trial and error. The person who seeks to lead a fruitful Christian life will have to endure much misunderstanding, much apparent failure, some temporary discouragement. But, because of the dynamic life within him, these setbacks will only serve to enlarge his understanding, challenge his perseverance, and direct him toward more fruitful possibilities. If his thinking is permeated by awareness of process, the moment of failure may be a moment of insight, a spur to new effort and greater achievement for Christ and neighbor.

31.

EXAMINING THE PREMISES

In buying a new house most people are sensible enough to examine the premises. To fail to do so would be to court the chance of getting a bad deal and perhaps a disastrous one. The wise buyer in examining the premises carefully scrutinizes the foundation upon which the house is built. The wise man buys a house built on rock. Others will eventually pay for their folly.

Without making too much of the pun, we can carry the analogy of examining the premises over to the less material phases of human life. But, all too often, materialistic, worldly prudence departs when ideas or moralities are offered for sale. Conclusions built on the shaky premises are accepted casually; indeed they are offered casually as though there were no need to establish their merit by a reasonable foundation.

Examine the conversations and proclamations that take place around you or in the media and you will see how readily pernicious attitudes are presented and accepted on the basis of gratuitous assumptions. There operates a sort of naive faith, which would be totally condemned if it appeared in the religious sphere.

Conversations at cocktail and other parties, even where committed followers of Christ are present, often assume that divorce, birth control, and perhaps abortions are acceptable practices to sophisticated people. If matters veer to specifically religious topics it is usually assumed that the Church makes harsh and unreasonable demands for money and that ecclesiastical favors can usually be obtained by the right sort of donation. Human "love" is presented as the justification for the violation of the sixth commandment and it would indeed be a surprise, if not a shock, to the assembled gathering if someone protested that love of God must come first. Such a person might well be written off as a religious fanatic. Lying to the insurance company is rarely questioned and the need to pull strings, even to the point of bribery, borders on unquestionable doctrine. Persons will actually boast as to how they perjured themselves to get out of a difficult situation, and there is no expectation of disagreement from any quarter. The assumption always is that these standards are the acceptable ones, the ones under which reasonable people operate and which no intelligent person can question. To challenge these assumptions, to dig into the validity of the premises upon which they were based, would be regarded as a social crime, warranting ex-communication from further social gatherings.

The unwarranted assumptions of the media are also flagrant and obvious upon a little reflection. It is assumed that the pursuit of superior status, superior beauty, superior health, superior wealth, is unquestionably and totally justified. Such efforts might, of course, be valid under certain circumstances but, as presented in the media, these objectives are based on and appeal to snobbism, greed, vanity, and general selfishness. The teaching of Christ that mankind should seek first the kingdom of heaven and its justice and all these things will be added, would be considered irrelevant and positively harmful. The struggling, or even poor, individual is encouraged to pursue at all costs a better car, a better television set, a better hair oil, a better dentifrice. The economically oppressed individual in the ghetto is made to feel that happiness in this life can only be obtained by gaining the economic symbols of the very class which may have oppressed him. And then what? Having reached the middle or upper middle class, how will he find fulfillment in his life? Apparently only by more of the same, at higher prices.

The whole advertising picture is shot through with a cynicism about human nature and motivation that appalls the person who believes, with the Bible, that true wisdom, growth in virtue, and union with God are basic to a fulfilled and meaningful life. The media, not only in advertising but also in plays and talk shows, often do not oppose this directly, but operate on the assumption that such values are of minor importance when compared with the "real business" of contemporary living.

Even in religious polemics, Christians in general, and Catholics in particular, are often too ready to grant the assumptions of their critics and opponents. The breast-beating of the sixties and seventies surely had some justification but, upon examination, it was tainted by smugness and superiority vis-à-vis the past. Must one accept the unqualified picture of an unending succession of bad popes, corrupt bishops, and callous priests without any reference to their exceptional circumstances, without any perpective on the humility and the persevering holiness of the majority of church-men and lay people? In modern trials, it is an imperative, almost to the point of exaggeration, that all sides of the case must be heard. Historically, as far as the Church is concerned, guilt is assumed in nearly all questionable cases. Then that guilt is expanded to include the whole Church—past and present.

It is one of the paradoxes of our time that the broad and often unwarranted condemnation of institutions is accompanied by the exculpation of individuals. Without a careful examination of a person's freely chosen attitudes and actions, it is assumed that he is simply the product of his heredity and environment. The criminal is not guilty; society is guilty. The neurotic aggressor who makes life intolerable for those around him is not responsible; his parents and home life shaped him into what he is. These appraisals may be true in many cases but are they to be assumed without examination? Does the element of free choice have nothing to do with the formation of an individual personality? Was not God's grace available to this individual? Was it not possible that he knew that he needed help and guidance and was unwilling to seek it out? Why was it that his brother from the same household developed into a humble and self-sacrificing Christian?

Perhaps it may seem more charitable to assume that all evil attitudes and actions derive from causes for which the individual is not responsible, but are we willing to say the same about good actions and good attitudes? Such an attitude about human nature renders it a sort of mechanical zombie. Free, responsible personhood tends to disappear from the earth, and we are left with rather uninteresting causes and effects. Fortunately some of our more astute psychologists are beginning to set aside the simplistic analyses of the past and to recognize that, despite neurotic and social forces, there are points in every human being's life when there is a rift in the clouds and the sunlight of truth makes possible an authentic choice for better or for worse.

To sum up this thought with a particular example: a man may not be responsible for being an alcoholic but he *may* (not always) be responsible for not accepting or seeking out the help he needs.

All of the above gives weight to our original contention: that it is important in religious and moral matters, as in everything else, to examine the premises, the foundation, upon which ideas, attitudes, institutions, movements and the like are based. A reflective mind, a critical mind, but most of all a mind positively committed to truth, not in isolation, but in its integrity, is essential to mature living. The first rule of human wisdom is openness to the truth; the second rule is to put the proposed "truth" in perspective and to understand the assumptions on which it is based.

In terms of our own personal spiritual life, going to the roots will often show us that some of our own thoughts and attitudes which we thought to be virtuous are actually rooted in pride, envy, or one of the other negative human drives. The spiritual examen of St. Ignatius Loyola, concentrating not so much on one's faults as on the roots of one's faults, can assist immeasurably in re-orienting one's life in Christian terms. Examining the premises, the roots, the foundations can save one from a life of falsity.

32.

ENCOUNTERING CHRIST

The Easter gospels have several instances of failure to recognize Christ at the first moment of encounter. Mary Magdalen perceived Christ as the gardener at first and only after gentle prodding did she recognize Him as the Master. The disciples on the way to Emmaus considered Him a stranger. Although they were moved by His words and His presence they did not realize that Christ had spoken to them until He disappeared after the breaking of the bread. At the Sea of Tiberias Peter and the others saw Him as an unrecognized figure on the shore. It was not until He enabled them to haul in a catch that they recognized that it was "the Lord."

These instances have many implications, but one in particular is suggestive for the purposes of this meditation. We are led to ask ourselves: "How often do we encounter Christ and fail to recognize Him at the time?"

Devout followers of Christ often miss His presence today in the liturgy. How often have you wondered after Mass, why you had hardly one moment that was fully conscious of God's presence in the eucharistic sacrifice and even in the eucharistic sacrament? Perhaps you came into the church without having tried to stir up the spirit of recollection. Then there was the problem of getting a suitable seat, finding the proper place in the missalette, glancing perhaps at the announcement sheet, all the while being conscious of others coming in and taking their respective positions. Then the Mass began and there was standing and sitting, and listening and responding, and movement on the altar, and the tone of voice of the priest, and his gestures, and the implications of his homily, and music, perhaps good or poor. All these elements seized your attention, which also resonated with some personal concerns which you brought with you from home or work, personal anxieties perhaps, about future commitments or simply about how the rest of the day would be spent. Where was the encounter with Christ in all this? Here was the supreme opportunity of the week to enter into full communion with Christ in common with your brothers in the Lord, yet after all was over, there seemed to have been hardly a second of conscious recognition.

The celebrant, too, can have the same problems and often greater ones. He must often feel like the disciples at Emmaus, who recognized Christ only after He had departed.

Even in so-called private prayer or meditation, how often there is little or no conscious contact with God! One has good intentions at the start but, because of failure to summon one's conscious energies, one fails to center attention. Ten or twenty minutes may pass in idle distractions. The experience seems like an almost deliberate avoidance of God rather than an effort to achieve communion. Sometimes this is unavoidable because of human weakness, but very often it may be the result of careless preparation, apathetic orientation, or self-centeredness. These lead us to treat the present Christ like a gardener.

Sermons are often delivered about encountering Christ in others. We hear the words of St. Matthew's Gospel: "Whatever you do to the least of My brethren, you do to Me." We are urged to raise our consciousness to a point where we recognize Christ in others and others in Christ and respond accordingly. Such a consciousness would of course give human relations a dimension, a saving lovingness which would enrich human lives profoundly. And yet the good Christian throws a coin in the beggar's hat in a distracted and dutiful spirit, or visits the sick in the hospital with a certain forced cheerfulness, followed by a welcome release from strain when the "job" is accomplished. Perhaps beforehand, perhaps later, the act of Christian love may be seen in its proper context. At the time, the circumstances and efforts consumed one's entire attention. The conscious encounter with Christ was lost in the mechanics of the operation. The spirit of recollection failed at the moment when it would have been most meaningful, most enriching to all concerned, most refreshing for the one who gave and the one who received. "Who gives himself with his gift feeds three—himself, his hungering neighbor and Me."

The lives of the saints are filled with supernatural revelations of Christ's presence in others, no doubt because the saints were *conscious* of meeting Christ in others. The story of St. Christopher is a classic example: the person he carries lovingly, turns into Christ Himself. Or the beggar who is helped, suddenly reveals the face of Christ. "The Vision of Sir Launfal," from which the above verse was quoted, is but one of many literary creations which remind us that the Lord is to be found in the very beggar at our gates. Yet how can we recognize Christ in others when our dulled consciousness refuses to recognize Him in ourselves? "If you love Me you will keep My word and My Father will love you and We will come to you and take up Our abode within you."

These thoughts are challenging to the superficiality and the distracted nature of our "post-Christian life." Committed Christians, who should be springing fountains of God's power, redeeming, strengthening not only themselves but others, lead a sort of two-dimensional life, mostly unconscious of the gift they bear. Or even if moments of consciousness are obtained, they are all too readily dissipated in the trivialities of insignificant "problems."

How then do we deepen and multiply encounters with Christ? To have deliberate forethought before entering into prayer, liturgical or otherwise, and before undertaking social relations of any type, charitable or otherwise, would be of primary importance. A general contemplative spirit must be nurtured through regular habits of meditation. There must also be a check-up after the event. At least the disciples at Emmaus recognized Christ and their experience of Christ after the event, so that all its fruit was not lost. Next time, we might assume, they would be more alert. The same may be true with us. Perhaps we can learn to recognize Him at once in the recital of the Scriptures and in the breaking of the bread.

Very often there will need to be a general preparation for encounter through a revised sense of proportion. This might be described as learning to value what should be valued and not to allow secondary considerations to assume a primary role in the acting out of life. We have to ask ourselves what is the real meaning and value of liturgical prayer, of private prayer, of sincerity, of life itself. Is there anything more important than encountering Christ and walking with Him and working with Him, than sharing Him with others, than living for Him? Is attendance at Mass the mere fulfillment of a duty, primarily a time to be gotten through, or is it a communal celebration of and renewal of Christ's saving death and resurrection in an act of solidarity which involves both oblation and communion, word and sacrament? The clarification of such perspectives and values can lead to more intimate encounter.

Many spiritual writers have spoken of the importance of doing what you are doing, that is to say, of entering wholeheartedly and with full consciousness into the total implications of your actions, including the act of being present or the act of encountering the Other. Do what you are doing, but at the same time allow God to do what He is ever doing: giving Himself to us. We should pray incessantly for the gift of openness to Christ-encounters.

33.

SOCIAL ACTION

When we reflect upon the Second Vatican Council's demands for social action and involvement on the part of devoted Catholics there are numerous lines of meditation which can help us to fulfill our role more effectively.

If we are to be the instruments of God in building a better world and thereby building up the Kingdom we must constantly keep in mind the opening words of Psalm 127: "Unless the Lord build the house, they labor in vain who build it." Unfortunately this warning is often the first thing forgotten once a communal project or organization is set in motion. The organizers and their recruits become so absorbed with the technology of promoting the work that the fact that it is primarily God's work and not theirs and that therefore it will be promoted primarily by God's deeds and not theirs, is not discarded but loses the centrality which it ought to have.

Emphasis on God's purposes and operation in a project does not minimize the importance of using appropriate instrumentalities to attain the end desired. God works through human means; He does not reject the created techniques of which He Himself is ultimately the author. So much is completely obvious. What is not so obvious, or at least not so much noticed, is that the Christian is seeking to perform not merely a natural but a supernatural work, one appropriate to those who have been called to be sons of God and co-heirs of Christ and who must have in mind the renewal of the world according to the principles of the gospel. Unless the individuals and group involved remember that they are operating as God's instruments, they may achieve a certain natural success, but it will inevitably have little relevance to building up the Kingdom of God on earth. What good is it to have magnificent hospitals, excellent organizations for the relief of famine, and zealous community groups determined to promote the welfare of all, if all this leads only to more selfishness, more pride, more worldliness, more indifference to God than previously? Works that are not permeated by Christian love, which are not motivated by Christian ideals, which are not supported by God's grace, are obviously of little value in nourishing men's spiritual relationship to God and man. Some of the techniques and methodologies, as well as the results attained, may distract both the actionists and the recipients from the realization of their total dependence on God. A certain pride in technical accomplishments, on the one hand, and a sort of critical demandingness, on the part of the recipient, can distract from the pure gift of God and the inner appreciation of God's loving concern. The sick patient in the technically perfect hospital may well consider himself the object of technique rather than the object of love. The loving communication of God has somehow been lost in the process.

One needs to reflect upon the activities of Mother Theresa of Calcutta and her group to perceive what authentic social action by Christians should really embody. She has healed not only bodies but persons, precisely because she has remembered the words of the psalm: "Unless the Lord build the house, they labor in vain who build it."

A second line of reflection is a variation or specification of the first. It is summarized in the words of John Donne: "No man is an island." Although it might be thought that the very fact that one participates in social activity would make such a reflection unnecessary, this is far from true. It really does not take much observation or experience to see that functionaries engaged in promoting the common good are often isolated within their own personalities, intent on moving material levers but reluctant to communicate themselves in the process. The fact that they are participating in social action at all is perhaps much to their credit, but it is not enough. God works through persons as instruments but not merely as mechanical instruments. He moves through persons according to the nature of personhood, which involves wisdom and understanding and love. The detached, impersonal administrator of the welfare agency, the school, the hospital, whatever it may be, is an anomaly in Christian terms. The same is true of rank-and-file workers—the teachers, the nurses, the doctors, the social investigators. When God works through someone He works through the most profound aspects of human nature elevated by grace, that is to say, primarily through the understanding and a loving heart. The cold, mechanical purveyor of communal services may have something of value to give but its value is deeply wounded by his failure to give himself. This is not the way of God and cannot promote His work among men suitably. "No man is an island." Those genuinely engaged in Christian social action know that the gift without the giver is bare. They know too that the beneficiaries of social action will be aided only temporarily and superficially unless they are aided on the level of their personhood. To know that this service is a gift of God in Christ, Who loves them to the very depths of their being—this is indeed great gain. It is a gain which can only be effective through those who, refusing to wall themselves off from others, embrace them as brothers.

A third line of reflection is related to the other two. It suggests that in the area of social action, even small initiatives, when imbued with the power and presence of God, can bring about unforeseen results of great magnitude. Negatively we have seen this disproportionate effect accomplished by small cadres of Communists in various parts of the world. Small but dedicated groups, seemingly dedicated to the welfare of the oppressed, concentrating their energies in vulnerable areas, have in moments of crisis been able to obtain incredible power over the community. If this is true of the Devil, how much more true must it be of God?

Again the example of Mother Theresa is relevant. Here we have one woman, with a small group of nuns surrounding her, who has captured the attention of the world and its admiration and support. Who can calculate the loving response of human hearts which have been stimulated by the example of her relatively small project in Calcutta? Her work is now spreading throughout the world; undoubtedly others will be led to follow her example. Even if only a few wretched persons are helped and healed in the streets of Calcutta this magnificent sign of Christ's love for men is bound to help and heal, however slightly, millions of others throughout the world.

God's power, when it is allowed to enter into and break through a human endeavor, fills us with wonderment and praise. If He told us that faith only the size of a grain of mustard seed could move mountains into the sea, how much more can a faith-filled work, however small in scope, accomplish in terms of moving the hearts of men into the sea of God's merciful love?

The lesson of these and similar reflections is clear enough: let no one move haphazardly and thoughtlessly into social action without deep meditation on its implications. Let no one expect to achieve fruitful results for God without the presence of God, without the love of God working in the hearts of his instruments, and without the realization that God's power and not man's acts will determine the extent and the depth of the outcome. "Unless the Lord build the house, they labor in vain who build it."

34

THROUGH HIM, WITH HIM, IN HIM

Guidance in prayer, too long neglected perhaps in pastoral counseling, is once more receiving needed emphasis. The pastoral counselor thus is filling at least in part the role once played by "the spiritual director." It is indeed an encouraging sign that devoted Christians are coming once again to realize the spiritual help which can be offered by a counselor of devotion and experience. Perhaps some of the spiritual writers of the past were over-insistent on the fact that one could not grow in the Christian life without such direction, but this could not mean that the total absence of direction is desirable either. As Cardinal Newman well said, normally God uses men not angels to promote His work on earth. Many false starts, false steps and wasted energies can be avoided with the assistance of someone who has already sedulously followed the genuine pathways to fruitful prayer.

An example of how inexperience or lack of awareness of the complexities of prayer can lead to a sort of spiritual dead-end is given in the following anecdote.

A man who had dedicated himself seriously to contemplative prayer even in the midst of a very active life found that although he had some moments of joy through his prayer he did not seem to be growing, at least consciously, into a deeper union with God. Finally he decided to consult a spiritual counselor. The following dialogue ensued:

Client: Father, I spend twenty minutes or so, morning and evening, every day, in trying to unite myself more deeply to God in prayer. I have been doing this for two years or more. I have found greater peace and greater faith, deeper hope and love. I am more aware of God during the distractions of daily life. But in spite of all this I feel that there must be something basically wrong with my approach to prayer.

Counselor: Why do you say that?

Client: Simply because I don't seem to have advanced in union with God much beyond the degree I attained very quickly after I began this form of prayer. I don't have the overwhelming sense of God's power and presence that I had hoped for. In my prayers God still seems rather remote, although I am conscious that He is there listening to me and helping me. To put it another way, I don't think I am fully tuned in. You know how it is when you turn on the radio and you are not quite on the station: there's a lot of static, and communication is distinguishable but not crystal clear. The analogy limps, of course.

Counselor: But you do feel that you are making some contact with God and that this contact is having a significant impact on your interior and exterior life?

Client: Undoubtedly. I am a much better Christian than I was two years ago but I seem to have reached a sort of dead end. I had thought that I might become more and more deeply united to God, more and more caught up in His love, more and more aware of being His loving instrument. This may sound a little pietistic, but I am telling you how I honestly felt.

Counselor: Suppose you tell me just a little bit about how you begin your prayer and how you carry it on.

Client: My prayer seems to correspond pretty well to what spiritual writers call the Prayer of Simplicity. I simply begin by placing myself in the presence of God. Then in a sort of imaginative, mystical way I place myself in the heart of Christ and offer myself in union with Him to the Father. I go out of myself, as it were, and in union with Jesus offer myself as an oblation. I call on the Holy Spirit to give me the spiritual energy to continue this act throughout the prayer. It is a totally outgoing, giving sort of process, which I had hoped would lead to an experience of union with God as its ultimate effect. However, I never seem to reach that goal, or at best only touch on it for a second.

Counselor: That is much in itself. But tell me this, is this your schema, the pattern of your approach throughout the entire period of prayer?

Client: Yes, more or less. But there are moments of distraction when I lose the thread. But by and large I am pressing forward and upward in active oblation that continues for the whole time of prayer.

Counselor: You must find praying a bit of a strain with all this pressing and offering and moving upward.

Client: Yes, I do at times but at other times I have a sense of calm, continuing strength, a sense that God accepts this oblation, even though He does not choose to admit me into the intimacy of directly experiencing Him.

Counselor: Perhaps you are trying to do all the work yourself by your own will power even though you are associating yourself with Jesus and His Holy Spirit. I don't mean to say that you are ruling out the importance of grace, but perhaps you are being overly aggressive in some respects so that the prayer is suffused more by your effort than by God's healing and strengthening presence. Perhaps I am not expressing myself well, but the analogy of the Mass might clarify the point I am trying to make.

Client: What do you mean by the "analogy of the Mass?"

Counselor: In the Mass those present unite themselves with Christ in His oblation to the Father. This is the consecration, the sacrificial offering. But the Mass does not end there. The oblation is followed by the communion. This is the action of the Mass in which the Father returns His glorified, redemptive Son to us in the gift of holy communion. This is the climax in which our oblation in Christ is rewarded and completed by the entrance of God in Christ into the intimacy of our being, filling us with His power and sustaining presence. The integrity of the Mass, in other words, calls for not only oblation but communion. And it is precisely this communion which seems to be lacking in your prayer.

Client: You mean my prayer is all one way, an oblation offered up to God without room for God's coming back to me in a sort of spiritual communion?

Counselor: It seems obvious, doesn't it, when you think about it? But you would be surprised how many people there are who make beautiful oblations of themselves but leave no time or room for God's return gift of Himself to fill the empty places in their hearts. You may inadvertently have been one of these people.

Client: What would you suggest then?

Counselor: Simply to follow the pattern I have already suggested. Your prayer up to now, although beautiful in itself, has been rather one-sided, really just half a prayer. I would suggest that you try now to divide your prayer into two parts: the oblation part, which you are already accomplishing, and then the communion part, whereby you open yourself up and call on God to fill your mind and heart like a great chalice into which He pours Himself—healing, strengthening, transforming. Thus, your prayer is not a one-way matter but a dialogue, a reciprocal relationship with God. Offering leads to response; oblation leads to communion. But to receive, you must be receptive, open, welcoming, in-gathering. . . .

It seems almost anti-climactic to say that the client in this instance experienced a notable improvement in his prayer life after having received the above advice. His intentions had been good all along. He had been following what he thought were valid procedures in prayer, but the experience had not been as fruitful as desired. The simple analogy of the action of the Mass enabled him to restructure his prayer life in a freshly transforming way. One might think that it was odd that he had never thought of this himself. He needed the guidance of an experienced counselor to help him. God wishes to be worshipped in spirit and in truth, and the true meaning and process of effective prayer sometimes require a light which, under God, only a loving and enlightened brother can give.

35

CONTRARIES

Some critics have maintained that Christianity is a series of contradictions. It would be better and more accurate to say that it is a life of contraries, which are nevertheless harmonized in a general synthesis.

To meditate on some of these contraries is often revealing, indeed helpful in understanding the richness of Christian teaching and its ability to encompass and to penetrate all aspects of human existence.

The two basic mysteries of Christian life, namely the Trinity and the Incarnation, are both defined in terms which lead some to call them contradictions but which, upon proper examination, reveal themselves as mysterious but not conflicting. The fact that there are three persons in one divine nature would only be a contradiction if it were maintained that there were three persons in only one person or three natures in only one nature. Such is not the case. What is revealed is a divine unity of nature which nevertheless is rich in threefold personality, a doctrine which communicates to the Christian believer not only the inner life of God but also an insight into the unity and diversity of God's creation. It throws a special light on why, although there are many human beings, they are called to be one in understanding and love.

The Incarnation reveals that in Christ there exists a human and divine nature but one person, a divine person, the Son of God. "The Word was made flesh and dwelt among us;" God has entered into human history and taken to Himself a nature like ours in everything but sin. He has identified Himself with every man and offered every man the opportunity to identify himself with God in Christ. Because of this identification with us He is able to offer His body and blood for man's redemption and at the same time give this sacrifice a divine value. His coming has drawn down the Holy Spirit of God upon us and given us a new relationship to the Father whereby in the words of St. Paul, we can say: "Abba." In the well-known axiom of St. Augustine: "God became man so that man might become God." When the priest takes wine and water into the chalice, mixing the two, he speaks of this ceremony as a sign of man's opportunity to participate in the divine nature as a result of the Incarnation. These apparent contraries— God and man—become harmonized through one mediator, Christ, both God and man. Apparent opposites are harmonized into a saving union with no loss of identity on either side. In this apparent paradox the whole life of grace, redemption, Sonship, and glorification opens up and becomes real, even comprehensible to a degree, although the mystery cannot yet be plumbed in its totality.

But there are numerous other apparent paradoxes, ambiguities, contraries, in Christian revelation and life. There is the church as the mystical body of Christ with Christ its head, with spotless holiness, doctrine, grace, and worship and yet with its very human shortcomings in terms of its members: the holy church, on the one hand, and the sinful church on the other, the sinfulness not residing in the church *per se* but in some of its individual components. At various times in history the emphasis, or rather overemphasis, on one element or the other has led either to triumphalism or pessimism or even contempt. It is the proper balancing and understanding of the "contrary" elements in the church which will give an authentic understanding of its meaning and history and therefore a more satisfactory appreciation of its value. In this case, as in the case of all the other "contraries" in the church, it is the distorted emphasis on one side or the other which frequently leads to disenchantment and even heresy.

The danger of distorted emphasis is particularly evident in the matter of body and spirit. The temptation has been to express this dualism in terms of the body *versus* spirit, whereas the authentic Christian teaching is of coordinates, distinct in many ways, contrary in certain respects, and yet harmonizable into the glorious unity of a knowing and loving being. The proponents of an extreme secular humanism have condemned the church for ignoring the rightful demands of the body in favor of what they describe as "pie in the sky" in some future life, while those imbued with the puritanical or manichaean temperament tend to disown the body and all its works.

But the Son of God took to Himself a human nature including a body, He fulfilled His life and death on earth in the body, He assumed the body into heaven after His glorious resurrection, and He now sits bodily at the right hand of God. In the matter of bodily needs He says "Seek ye first the kingdom of God and His justice and all these things shall be added unto you." In genuine Christianity there is no rejection of the body; the body shares in God's glorification and man's salvation. The apparent opposite poles are integrated and caught up in a redeemed world where not a sparrow falls without the Father's knowledge and the hairs of everyone's head are all numbered. Some persons who condemn Christianity for ignoring the body reject in the same breath the doctrine of the resurrection of the body. Part of the blessedness of our Christian faith is that we see richness in every moment of human living because of man's total redemption, body and soul.

What has just been said highlights the "now—hereafter" contrary which, as we have said, some would interpret as rejection of the now in favor of the hereafter. The truth is that Christians believe that the eschatological era has begun with the coming of Christ. Through grace, life is now supernatural in itself and in its orientation; "now" takes on a new importance, a new value, because it is a moment of entrance into the eternal now. Every moment on earth is valuable, in being an opportunity to unite more deeply with the eternal God, beginning now and continuing for eternity. Neither now nor hereafter is slighted by Christian living; both are enriched.

Other pairings which at first seem contradictory, when properly understood reveal a breathtaking harmonization of the complexities of human life. Christ speaks frequently of peace: "My peace I give unto you." But He also speaks of coming not to give "peace but the sword." Only a simplistic mind, unaware of the totality of the gospels, can find a contradiction here. Christian peace is gained not by an apathy or unconcerned passivity but by zealous pursuit of God's glory and man's salvation, using the weapons of faith, hope, and love, which, although in themselves healing, may occasion terrifying pain, misunderstanding, and martyrdom. But for all that, the battle will not cease to be waged, for what is sought is a peace of life not a peace of empty death.

Although meekness and fortitude may seem to be contrary there is no contradiction between them. Nor is fortitude merely passive and enduring; it involves great positive efforts, great forward movement in the face of obstacles and even enemies. But its motives are loving ones and its means are equally loving. If by turning the other cheek and praying for enemies it pours coals of fire upon their heads it is only so they may know they are being burned and may emerge purified. But meekness will never allow evil to triumph; because it is a Christian virtue it is dedicated to and motivated by the supreme virtue of charity—which means in effect that it will always be dominated by the widest possible understanding of that which gives glory to God and confers blessings on others. It does not destroy fortitude but it enlightens it so that it may serve the loving purposes of the God of love.

One could meditate endlessly on the profound insights available in the pairing of Christian "contraries." Such reflections teach us that Christianity is simple but not simplistic, that it gathers together all complexities of life in a radical harmony, leaving out nothing, embracing everything, and lifting all up in an integrated thrust to the heart of God.

36

FAVORABLE PRESUMPTIONS

There is a place for negative thinking, even among Christians. There is such a thing as too much zeal, which in the long run is self-defeating and needs a curb by reflection on the evil results of "over-doing it." Although Christian emphasis must necessarily be on love it must also take account of the obstacles to love and resist and eliminate them. Followers of Christ are characterized by hope but this does not rule out a practical realism which weighs obstacles carefully as well as the available means that will overcome them. Although the Christian mind is favorable in general to new projects designed to improve the lot of mankind and to build up the kingdom of God on earth, it is also conscious of St. Paul's warning that many things are good but not all things are expedient. By and large, the joyful and hopeful Christian spirit will stress creative possibilities and mankind's call to richer and more satisfying living but it will not ignore the dark side of things, including common weaknesses in the present condition of human nature. It will put the most favorable light on human motivation but cannot disregard the findings of psychologists, as well as of spiritual directors over the centuries, that a large measure of human conduct is tainted at least to some degree by egotism.

But the mentality created by the gospel is largely one of positive thinking. It will have no truck with the pessimists of our time, who look upon human life as an absurdity, who cynically scoff at all claimants to altruism, or who live by the axiom that if anything bad can happen, it will. The genuine gospel attitude also finds itself in conflict with Jansenistic Christians who consider the human race to be so intrinsically steeped in sin that little can be expected from them except the possibility that, by divine power, they "may not always be as bad as they usually are."

No, genuine Christianity loves to re-echo the teachings of the gospel about joy, Sonship, love, new life in Christ, the power of the Holy Spirit, and the like. Although redemption from sin and initial conversion of mind and heart to God are foundational they are not the whole emphasis of divine revelation. These unquestionably important movements open up to the positive growth, the living out of the full implications of what it means to be baptized into Christ. The negative elements are present, but even they are positive in the sense that they involve a turning to God, a moving forward through His strength, a reaching out and an opening up to the abundant life of grace. Good Friday was necessary, but as everyone knows, its fulfillment is found in the new life of Easter morning. It is the Easter life into which the Christian has entered by his incorporation into the mystical body of which Christ is the head.

This creative, life-giving, enhancing spirit will lead the Christian to live in what might be described as an atmosphere of favorable presumptions. This involves a constructive, hopeful approach. The presumption always yields to the facts, yet the hopeful Christian does not anticipate negative factors as a matter of policy.

This notion of favorable presumptions is revealed in the Christian's attitude towards his fellow man. It is based on the teachings of Christ Himself, Who warned us against seeing the mote in our neighbor's eye and failing to take account of the beam in our own. Long before Anglo-Saxon law, the sincere Christian had learned to give the presumption of innocence to his neighbor. "Judge not, lest ye be judged." He knew that only God could see the inner motivations of man and that therefore only God was to be his judge. Such an attitude leads to an immediate bond of unity and acceptance whereby, since the innate dignity and the merit of others are acknowledged, others are treated as objects of veneration rather than of suspicion. With such a frame of mind the heavy pessimism which sometimes characterizes human life is immediately lifted and one lives in an atmosphere of presumed if not actual innocence. Although this may appear naive in view of the evil in men's hearts and the history of crimes against God and humanity, it is the only approach which can make life endurable individually or indeed socially.

But it has an even greater logic than this because it affirms man's essential goodness and the foreignness of evil to the human order as intended by God. It further implies the redemptive action of God in Christ whereby all men have been called to Sonship through grace made available for that purpose. Although the presumption of innocence may often be mistaken, it has a purifying effect both upon the object and the subject. Like praying for one's enemies, it heaps coals upon the heads of the guilty, coals which may in time burn away impurities.

The Christian mentality also makes favorable presumptions about the future. Christ Himself advocated this when He warned against solicitude for the morrow, saying, "the morrow will take care of itself." God gives us the strength to live each moment at a time, each moment as it comes. We do not have the strength today to live through the problems of tomorrow; that strength will come as it is needed. Therefore to create imaginative pictures whereby we are encountering problems and difficulties which we do not here and now have the means to bear is a form of absurdity. As Christians, however, we do know that we shall have the grace we need as the need arises. We know that we shall always be able to do God's will. That should be enough for favorable presumptions about the future.

Such an attitude is soundly enriching in terms of our present energies. Relieved of burdensome and unproductive worries we can devote ourselves wholly to whatever it is that God wills for us at this moment. Only the person given to negative presumptions about the future, realizes how much anguish, time, and energy have been involved in useless anxieties, over the course of a lifetime. Capacities for good have been markedly limited by capacities for anticipating evil. The favorable presumption of the Christian regarding the future pulverizes the burden of worry and releases fruitful sources of power for good.

Favorable presumptions regarding one's self are also significant factors for strength in the Christian life. Although such presumptions can be abused, still the mounting volume of self-hatred in the contemporary world makes it important to cultivate affirmative attitudes about one's self. Of course, we are not speaking of sinful presumption, which is in effect a calling upon God to approve of one's evil doing. The presumptions of which we speak are those that recognize God's love for us and our consequent right, indeed obligation, to love ourselves. Moreover, this attitude will extend the presumption of innocence even to one's self. Don't assume mortal sins which are not *certainly* so. And if one has failed in the past, one nevertheless assumes that God will help one not to fail in the future. That one is in the friendship of God is taken as a practical norm, apart from known mortal sin. That God's strength is ever available is taken for granted.

This last is not merely an assumption or presumption. It is a certainty of faith.

37.

MARY AND PURITY

Mary and purity? The theme is almost banal. The notion of Mary's intercessory power in the attainment of Christian purity has been preached so often and accepted so widely among Catholics that it has tended to become a pious assumption, honored with the lips, and yet, in many cases, not truly accepted for its existential relevance. It has become something like the notion that God is good. Everyone agrees, yet the thought may well have little direct influence on conduct. Our tendency is to say yes, and then go on to other things without any deep personal realization of the authenticity of the truth involved. This superficializing of certain basic Christian truths is something that must be frequently combatted both by ardent meditation and by acting out the reality of the doctrine in personal concrete terms.

The historical fact is that for those who truly value this truth about Mary's influence on purity, the power and effectiveness of her intercession are confirmed again and again. The saints, of course, never cease to report Mary's purifying influence in their own lives, but many rank and file Catholics with particular temptations in the area of sexuality can and do give striking testimony to the healing strength which can be obtained through her.

Every retreat master has an ample stock of examples in this area. One might too readily assume that they are pious fables created to make a point. They seem almost too good to be true. This is precisely the reason why so many have failed to take

actual advantage of Mary's force for purity, which is readily available for the asking. "Too good to be true." Like so many things
in Catholic tradition, Marian intercession gives rise to scepticism
because people cannot believe that such great effects can be
accomplished so easily. But the extraordinary thing is that it *is*
true: prayer to Mary can be a sovereign source of resistance to
sexual temptation and of strengthening the Christian vocation
to chastity whether within marriage or without.

One illustration among a million is that of the young boy of
adolescent years tormented by frequent impulses to violate the
Sixth Commandment. At the time he turned to Mary he had already been entrapped in habits of sexuality which were threatening to destroy his peace of mind and his whole Christian commitment. As a result of sermons which he heard on the subject and
the example of others whom he respected and admired he began,
in a sort of desperation, to say the rosary every day for the attainment of the grace of chastity. This was the turning point. Not
only was he able, with comparative ease, to overcome his lustful-
ness but his whole Christian life was deepened to the point of
genuine holiness.

A mature and sophisticated man of middle years unexpectedly
found within himself a revival of adolescent passions and desires,
threatening to undermine the whole structure and spiritual seri-
ousness of his life. Erotic fantasies and consequent stirrings toward
illicit sexual satisfaction became an almost obsessive torment in
his daily life. Even though he had always prayed to Mary for the
gift of purity, he realized that this prayer had become so routine
as to be almost meaningless in terms of his own inner convictions
about her power to assist. Summoning up sincerity and trust, he
placed all his mind and heart in the act of prayer, with immediate
results. The temptations did not disappear instantly but there was
a gradual mitigation, and all the while he felt that he had the grace
never to waver in his determination. He said only three Hail
Marys a day for this purpose but it was enough, because his heart
was in it. As is well known, the Mother of God cannot resist a
sincere petition.

As has been said, examples are endless. Everyone can find one or more either in his own life or in the experience of his acquaintances. Experience overwhelmingly supports the actuality of the church's position: prayer to Mary works; the grace to preserve or to restore chastity can be attained through her intercession.

The present need for a strengthening of purity is so obvious as not to need emphasis. The problem is not merely that of the particularized forms of pornography which besmirch the horizon but the constantly lowered atmosphere in which even devout persons are required to live. This debased atmosphere, in terms of sexuality, inevitably seeps into the thoughts and attitudes even of those who hold purity in highest esteem. One simply has to ask himself today: Am I not far more tolerant of obscene language, immodest attire, sexualized books, entertainment, and advertising than I was ten or fifteen years ago? Those who can give a negative answer to this are indeed blessed, almost exceptional. The erosion of standards in this area of the public forum has almost necessarily tended to weaken private resistances.

Those who are dedicated to truth, and especially the truth of the gospel of Christ, have to make a conscious effort to restore a proper sense of proportion regarding the place of sexuality in human life. Obviously there has been adolescent exaggeration which seems to give a supreme, all-encompassing value to mere physical acts, which, upon reflection, should be placed very far down on the scale of human gifts and values. Granted that sexual actions are necessary for the continuation of the race and as an ultimate expression of mutual love in marriage, they are only significant if they are in the service of love and life, and not substitutes therefor. Devotion to Mary helps to put sex in its proper perspective.

The basis for her effectiveness is her relationship to her Son, Who is purity incarnate. Devotion to her, therefore, creates a wholesome atmosphere surrounding the one who is her client. Walking in the presence of such a mother, how could an individual give way to lustful disorder? As mother, she continues to bring forth her Son in the hearts of her petitioners. And where

Christ is, there is purity, purity incarnate. Because of her relationship to Him, she has the intercessory power to gain special graces, to preserve innocence in the first place or to restore it if it has been lost. Because God in her Son makes all things new, even the person steeped in years of lust, can enter upon a life of dazzling innocence through the recreative power of the Spirit of Christ.

Mary's effectiveness for purity is appropriate to her role as mother. The mother is the great healer of her children. So, Mary by her influence can help to initiate and continue a healing process whereby the past wounds of lust are washed away and strength is communicated to resist the effect of new and unexpected viruses.

Just as a mother is instrumental in maintaining or restoring peace within the family, knowing how to harmonize all elements in a bond of unity, so this mother, Mary, is adept at obtaining graces which will penetrate even to the depths and hidden corners of the human psyche, overflowing even into the physical substratum; this can bring about a harmony within the individual whereby his sexual energies are caught up and transfigured in a general movement toward the fulfillment of God's will.

Most of all, she herself is an example of such harmony. Her assumption into heaven is proof that, by the grace of Christ, body and soul may be united in a peaceful oblation to the Father.

38.

FEEDING ON CHRIST

The notion of God as Shepherd is familiar to all who read the Scriptures. The famous psalm of the Old Testament beginning with the words "The Lord is my shepherd, there is nothing I shall want" has been loved by Jew and Christian alike for millenia. The shepherd, of course, provides for his flock; he is primarily the one who sees to their proper nourishment so that they can live and live abundantly.

Not surprisingly Christ, the divine Son, calls Himself the Good Shepherd. God in Christ feeds the flock in a new way with a new food, nourishing them in a new life. Israel had manna in the desert; Christ gives Himself as the bread of heaven. God the Good Shepherd has always fed the flock but in Christ He nourishes them with the bread of heaven that they may be truly sons of God and heirs of heaven.

Meditation on the sixth chapter of St. John's Gospel offers rich insights into Christ as the new supernatural nourishment of mankind. "I am the bread from heaven . . . he who eats My flesh and drinks My blood has everlasting life and I will raise him up on the last day." "The bread which I shall give is My life for the world."

Christ the Good Shepherd feeds His flock with a nourishment previously unknown, nourishment which gives life and gives life abundantly both here and hereafter. The Eucharist is this nourishment par excellence. No wonder the poet cries out: "O, bread of heaven, beneath this veil thou dost my very God conceal." The liturgical Eucharist is to be divided daily to the end of time, for the Shepherd, the Good Shepherd, will not leave His flock untended or unfed. Nor is it a question merely of avoiding starvation; He is concerned about nourishing up His flock to the fullness of their potential life.

Devout followers of Christ have always known that it was by means of the Eucharist that they were made capable of living fully Christian lives. Now, it is not even necessary for the preacher to urge weekly communion; the very power of Christ's nourishing presence has drawn the multitudes to the altar rail. Those who have received the call and the grace to partake of the bread of life daily, understand that this is the most important source of strength in their lives. Looking back perhaps on their less than devout pasts, they wonder how they could have failed to take full advantage of the enriching banquet of the Lamb of God. They have come to know what it means to live by Christ, and understand Him as that Person giving their life meaning, purpose, and possibility for expansion in a truly spiritual manner. "O sacred banquet in which Christ is consumed!"

Sometimes Catholics find their faith challenged by the tremendous mystery of the Eucharist. The temptation runs something like this: "Is it possible that the omnipotent God has willed that His divine Son be present under the appearances of bread and wine? Doesn't such a concept smack of pagan mystique? Is it possible for a sophisticated modern person to believe that under the sign of bread he is receiving Jesus Christ, body, blood, soul and divinity? Does not such a sacramental notion tend to degrade God and to depart seriously from the great reality of God as sublime, transcendent, ineffable, infinite, inscrutable?"

Such people are threatened by the daring nature of the eucharistic gift, the humility of God revealed therein, and the incredibility of a personal encounter with the Infinite in such a mundane form. But, from questioning the Eucharist, it is one step to questioning the Incarnation itself. Most of the arguments against the Eucharist can be directed against the very idea of God entering into human history, taking to Himself a human nature like to ours in everything but sin. "And the word was made flesh and dwelt amongst us." Indeed this, as well as the Eucharist, can be a hard saying if one is not totally open to grace. Some of Christ's disciples turned away and walked no more with Him after He had proclaimed Himself the bread of heaven. Then He turned to Peter and the other apostles and said: "Will you too go away?" Their reply has resounded through the centuries on the lips of the faithful: "Lord, to whom shall we go? Thou has the words of eternal life. And we have known and have believed that Thou are the Christ, the Son of God."

But actually a little reflection should show that the apparent challenge of the Eucharist need not be as great as it seems. Jesus said to His followers: "I have a meat which you know not: to do the will of Him Who sent Me." In other words He lived by the will of His Father; He was united to the Father; He lived by the Father. "I and the Father are One."

What better sign could there be that we live by Christ and with Christ and in Christ, sharing his Sonship with respect to the Father, than the human sign of bread which nourishes human life? He said: "Without Me you can do nothing." St. Paul said: "I live now, not I but Christ lives in me." And indeed at the Last Supper, in which the Eucharist was established, Jesus said to his followers: "If you love Me you will keep My word and My Father will love you and We will come to you and take up Our abode with you."

If you profess to be a Christian, then, you profess to live by Christ. It is His word which nourishes your mind, which provides your motivation, which instructs you in God's will and how to achieve it both here and in eternity. If you profess Christ, it means that you recognize the supernatural life of Sonship as a gift unattainable by merely human powers. It calls therefore for the gift of God's grace, Christ's grace which is communicated by Him through the Holy Spirit. It is impossible therefore to live as a co-heir with Christ without nourishment in His life and light.

These realities are signified and effected through the spiritually nourishing sacrament of the Eucharist in which communion with God in Christ is made possible by the power of the Spirit, who proceeds from the Father and the Son. The Eucharist then is the perfect sign of Christ as the bread from heaven that communicates Himself to God's holy people, nourishing them, as the good shepherd nourishes his flock, in all that they need to live the life to which they are called in time and eternity. The Eucharist is the supreme sacrament since it signifies and in a way renews and extends the graces of all the other sacraments. It expresses the very essence of the Christian life, namely the fullest possible union with Christ attainable in this life.

The Christian is of course nourished by the Gospel, by the other sacraments, by every act of charity, by the example of the saints and holy ones—but all this nourishment is caught up, expressed, enlarged in the sacrament which has been described by Vatican II as the source and summit of Christian life, that is to say the Eucharist.

In the light of such reflections, how can the Eucharist seem unreal, unsuitable, inappropriate as a medium of God's encounter with men in terms of their sanctification? How can it be surprising that what is signified is truly communicated, truly present under the sign? God's gifts of Himself are not empty shells, mere symbols, but realities, indeed the deepest realities of existence. When God *signifies* His presence, He *is* present. And when He *signifies the gift* of Himself, He *gives* Himself. Authentic Christian tradition and experience have always confirmed what the Bible teaches, that God in Christ is truly, really, and substantially present under the Eucharistic signs. How could it be otherwise since Christ is the Good Shepherd who nourishes His sheep, not with merely human food but with His own divine life? "I am the bread of life."

39

HOW PERFECT IS PERFECTION?

To the modern mind the accepted notion of Christian perfection is rather frightening. Probably there is no more effective way to "turn off" a group of young people than to tell them that they are expected to be perfect. "How can anyone be perfect?" they exclaim. "The whole idea is unrealistic."

Nor are the critics limited to youth. Many an old-timer, even among Catholics, will say: "One thing I never could buy is this notion that everyone is expected to be perfect. It just isn't possible, human nature and the world being what they are."

But when the retreat master or the missioner quotes the words of Christ in the fifth chapter of St. Matthew's Gospel: "Be ye perfect even as your Heavenly Father is perfect," committed Christians, because of their faith, will not deny this, although in practice they may tend to overlook it. They are likely to regard it as just one more of those mysterious sayings which perhaps were not intended to be carried out literally.

Some extreme notions of Christian perfection set forth by certain spiritual writers might well lead the rank and file of Christians to the brink of despair. Perhaps this is unfair to spiritual writers; very often they are setting forth a goal to be aimed at rather than an absolute achievement. Some commentators say: "Better to aim too high than too low. Relative perfection consists in moving towards the good with all one's potentialities. The absolute attainment will come only at the end, in the beatific vision."

Some people have the impression that the stress on Christian perfection requires that they be at the highest level of every virtue; in other words, that they be absolutely perfect even in this life. Such is of course impossible and was not achieved even by the greatest saints.

The tendency of this sort of thinking is to place every virtue on a par. This can only lead to a lesser achievement in the more important virtues because human energies, even elevated by grace, can be spread too thin. In addition, this sweeping sort of perfectionism leads to a negative approach whereby one is always concerning one's self about the slightest defect in any area of life. Attention is withdrawn from the positive development and growth of the theological virtues of faith, hope, and charity, and a sort of petty scrupulosity may easily develop. Indeed some psychologists feel that perfectionism of this type is merely rooted in a sort of pride or glory-seeking which mistakenly assumes that the individual should be in a state of divine perfection rather than in a struggle to make his way forward, with many mistakes, setbacks, and disappointments.

Many good Christians try to simplify the notion of perfection by saying that it consists in always trying to do God's will, whatever that may be. Although there is much truth in this assertion, it perhaps borders on an over-simplification. It tends to equate perfection with one's own efforts to the extent that the individual may, unconsciously at least, minimize the reality of God's gift of Himself in grace, which is the authentic source of holiness. Such a concept is not always particularly helpful in solving the difficulties of discovering God's will in complex situations. Nor is it able clearly to delineate the intensity of fervor or the nature of the priorities which should be appropriate in every situation. Moreover such an emphasis can readily give rise to a kind of legalistic approach to virtue whereby the individual, instead of being God's friend and instrument, becomes His servile subject, whose only concern is to avoid earning the displeasure of his Master.

What then of the "holiness for all" called for by Christ and the whole Christian tradition, including the most recent Council?

Several things should certainly be taken into account. The first of these is that the statement of Christ about perfection at the opening of this meditation is paralleled in St. Luke's Gospel by the words: "Be ye merciful as your Heavenly Father is merciful." This should at least give us a clue as to where the emphasis lies in the pursuit of perfection. Mercy is a form of love in action and it would be accurate to say that the height of Christian perfection is in charity. St. Paul, as everyone knows, speaks in First Corinthians of charity as the "more excellent way." "And if I should have prophecy and should know all the mysteries, and all knowledge, if I should have all faith, so that I could remove mountains and have not charity, I am nothing." The charity of which he speaks is primarily the love of God in Christ, a charity which then overflows into the embracing of all God's children. This charity to one's brother is worthless unless it is God-oriented: "And if I should distribute all my goods to feed the poor, and if I should deliver my body to be burned, and have not charity, it profiteth me nothing." Christ Himself summarized perfection in His twofold commandment: to love God with all one's heart and one's neighbor as one's self. And He qualified this even further by His "new commandment:" that His followers should love one another as He had loved them—which was of course even unto self-emptying and death.

The matter of priorities in perfection is clearly established in terms of the faith that worketh through charity. This charity is not a mere stressing and straining toward good by the individual through his own efforts; it is an opening out to the Spirit who is poured forth into the hearts of the faithful and who moves them to loving service of God and neighbor. The Christian in pursuit of perfection must first have his heart open in charity and then other virtues will follow in due course. "If you love Me you will keep My commandments." Charity dominates, permeates and motivates all other phases of the Christian life. St. Paul spells it out: "Charity is patient, is kind; charity envieth not, dealeth not perversely; is not puffed up; is not ambitious, seeketh not her own, is not provoked to anger, thinketh no evil" etc. It is not a question of concentrating one's primary attention on little faults but on the great, affirmative, transforming gift of love.

Sometimes the pursuit of charity can have as a side-effect a momentary distraction from perfection in marginal areas. St. Theresa of Avila remarked at one point that although as Superior, she was committing many more faults than in her sheltered life, she was also accomplishing much greater things for the love of God. Since charity by its very nature involves God's people in large and daring enterprises, it may sometimes run ahead of the individual's ability to make adaptations called for by the new circumstances of launching out into the deep. But in time, charity catches up all aspects in God's encompassing love.

Finally, in reflecting upon where the emphasis should lie in the pursuit of Christian perfection, one should not fail to consult the experience of the Christian people down through the ages. Whom do the Christian people, indeed even the non-Christian people, regard as the most perfect? Is it the person with seemingly perfect self-control, the one who never loses his temper, who always seems to do the correct thing at the correct moment, who always does just what is expected of him, who gives little or no trouble to others, who responds with perfect courtesy and a sincere interest to the demands made upon him or her? Or is it the loving, burning, charitable heart, the loving person who, despite numerous faults perhaps, radiates the consuming love of Christ and embraces others without thought of himself, emptying, emptying, giving, giving, warm with sympathy, alive with concern, overflowing with mercy? The answer is simple and clear. "Charity covers a multitude of sins."

40

A LITTLE BIT GOES A LONG WAY

Although Catholic tradition prides itself on its great number of saints, there is, generally speaking, even among devout members of the church, little if any thought that they too might attain the heights of sanctity. Sanctity is considered something too remote and exceptional to be attainable in the ordinary course of ardent Christian living. Many would even think it a sin of presumption to entertain the thought of sanctity. No doubt there might well be such an element in the pursuit of sanctity for its own sake, or, to put it another way, the pursuit of sanctity for the satisfaction of one's perfectionistic ego.

Most people would judge that God calls saints just as he calls priests and nuns to their particular vocations. Most of us are called to various levels of Christian holiness, they would say, even though our responses may not always be as generous as God would desire. But sanctity, no. That would require a heroism beyond normal powers, even normal powers elevated by normal grace. Moreover, the saints' lives have often been marked by miraculous occurrences, visions, discernment of spirits and the like, which must clearly come directly from God and usually bring with them tasks and duties beyond the scope of ordinary Christian mortals.

Such considerations are generally centered on canonized saints and these, as everyone knows, although large in absolute numbers, are extremely few in proportion to the Christian masses of history. Even though some spiritual writers have stated that the only mistake a Christian can make in life is *not* to be a saint, most of us would nod in appreciation of the epigram but feel that it has little relevance to our situation.

What then of sanctity in the more generic sense, the sense in which St. Paul described the recipients of his epistles? An argument can be made for the fact that any person in the state of grace is a saint in the broad sense. He is sanctified by union with God and the presence of God within him. Surely this is sanctity of a kind. And if the further assumption is made that the person in question has continuing good will, openness to God in his life, a desire for at least some growth in Christian living, he might even more aptly be described as a saint in this wider sense. This contention would be readily admitted by all; it would be impossible to deny that every Christian is called to sanctity in this way.

But there is a problem for many people even in this modified definition of sanctity, at least in terms of their carrying it out in their own lives. This centers on the notion of "growth." Having attained a certain intensity of prayerfulness and purity of motivation, a certain structure of good habits, they tend to feel that there is no room for further development except in terms of the normal accretion of time, with its piling up of merit. Such people turn away from the vision of new challenges; they feel incapable of making new efforts. Their concept of the Christian life is more of the same, with nothing new or different. Having pushed themselves, as they feel, to the limit, they see no beckoning from distant horizons. New Christian deepenings, involvements, when presented from the outside, strike them with horror. There comes a point when everything, anything, in the way of new action seems too much to undertake. Although Jesus said that His yoke was sweet and His burden light, they would agree with this only up to a point.

Such persons need to meditate more deeply on the power and the joy that Christ confers on those who try to live the more abundant Christian life. But they should also reflect upon the fact that new efforts are often far more burdensome in the anticipation than they are in the actual carrying out.

A few examples of how modest efforts can produce great fruits might be helpful in such a meditation.

There was a teacher in a high school who was known for his

tremendous influence for good on his students. This teacher was not extraordinary either in knowledge or personal gifts. In fact he was a rather quiet and retiring man. But he always made it a point to say a friendly, warm word to each student as often as possible. Nothing profound was said but he was able to communicate to them his genuine interest in them and his valuing of them as sons of God. Surely this was a small thing, well within the abilities of any teacher, but its effectiveness was tremendous in leading students to come to him voluntarily for guidance in their problems and to set him up as a model upon which their own lives could be patterned. In this area a little bit goes a long way.

There was a college professor who was known for his fascinating lectures in history. He seemed ultra-sophisticated. He was extremely witty and he made the dry facts of history dance engagingly in the front of the classroom. One day he pulled a handkerchief out of his pocket and a rosary fell to the floor. His secret life of prayer and devotion was exposed in that brief second. It gave a new dimension to his already great influence over the students. They realized as never before that wit and sophistication and knowledge and ability were not incompatible with a devoted spiritual life. His example would remain with them for their lives. A small event was to bring significant spiritual results.

In some cases it is just a matter of priming the pump. A person may be deeply troubled, even depressed, because of some loss in his life. One friend makes just a little extra effort to go out of his way to console him, to share his burden if only for a moment. This simple act of charity is enough to set in motion the forces of recovery. A genuine act of sympathy has become the turning point in the direction of more joyous and courageous living.

Examples could be multiplied, not only on the individual but on the community level where one small, loving voice at the right time has been the occasion of radical transformation.

This may offer a new perspective on growth in holiness. A very little bit can go a long way. Easy does it, when God works through us.

41

SICK AND BLIND

Have the liberalized reinterpretations of Scripture, theology, and church discipline since Vatican II succeeded in placing more or less pressure on the faith of Catholics? This is indeed a fine point and one which perhaps cannot be answered in generalities. Although it might be safe to say that the general loosening of rigidities has made it easier for modern man to believe in the church and in its teachings, those who are congenitally sceptical or who have a somewhat neurotic tendency to doubt may well have found new reasons for disquiet and uncertainty.

After all, the semi-compulsive doubter is a perennial phenomenon. Whether particular doctrines are easy or hard to believe may have some minimizing or maximizing influence on his dubiety, but his problem will remain nevertheless. The very nature of human existence is such that there are always new questions that may be raised, new difficulties to be answered. And this is all the more true in the area of a religion based on the special supernatural intervention of God in human history. There comes a time even in the most liberalized theological atmosphere when the mystery of God's dealings with men cannot be rationalized, or explained as though it were not a mystery but merely a problem to be solved, like any other problem, by purely human analysis. It is when such mysteries impinge upon our questioning and perhaps reluctant souls that the doubting Thomas in us all is likely to emerge from the shadows.

For those for whom this emergence is occasional, remedial measures are well-known and readily available. Prayer, meditation on the firm basic verities, advice of a counselor, the directing of the mind to other concerns until the pressure of the conflict has subsided, the studying of reliable modern commentaries on the problem involved: these are accepted measures for relieving doubt. Connected with this is the needed determination, the "will to believe," despite all temporary indications to the contrary.

Unfortunately, however, there are many persons to whom storms of doubt are not occasional but habitual. Devout followers of Christ and members of the church though they be, they may lead lives of continuous torment, where every passage of Scripture raises seemingly unanswerable objections, every sermon is a suggestion to disbelieve, every liturgical exercise a temptation to scoff, and every pronouncement of the church a goad to rebellion. Often, as these seizures come on, the individual is equally tortured by the fear that he is permanently losing his faith or that he has sinned gravely against God. There are periods of quiet in between, when all seems well, but then, often unexpectedly, some chance remark or everyday situation will trigger the entrance of extraordinary difficulties against the faith. And, if the person is given to much reading, he soon finds that even the most innocent-appearing novel or biography or essay is like a mine-field containing booby traps designed to destroy his faith. In anguish he must call out again and again with the man by the wayside: "Lord, I believe. Help Thou my unbelief."

For some people such agony may continue for years, perhaps even for a lifetime, but undoubtedly there are many others who, in the course of the development of their Christian life, go through such trials for a shorter period, although at the time they have no way of knowing what the duration will be. It is important, therefore, to reflect upon measures which may be helpful in relieving the faith-destroying effect of these tribulations.

A devout Catholic man recently explained how he had lessened the pressure of such difficulties.

"With great reluctance," he said, "I accepted the fact that I was sick in the area of faith. The continuing arousal of doubt, even though I intended to be and willed to be a believing Catholic, made me realize that there was something operating in me that was not appropriate or normal. When I discussed my difficulties with a friend he commented casually that not even St. Thomas Aquinas would have been capable of solving my difficulties if they were thrown at him in a second of time where he had to make an immediate answer. I realized that this was what I was trying to do: to handle profound and indeed staggering problems off the cuff, so to speak, as they came to me in church, in prayer, in the course of daily life. To handle them at all, however inadequately, it was necessary to take my mind off everything else, to interrupt normal operations. This, of course, created an impossible situation. My mind and soul were in constant turmoil.

"Having assured myself then that I was faith-sick, I resolved not to deal with the questions directly at all. I argued that just as a man with a broken leg cannot walk without immediately falling to the ground, so I must remain in the state where I was and not allow fresh difficulties to draw me out into the field of combat, since I would not have strength to fight. I resolved that I would simply turn away from the difficulties presented. I would merely say to myself that perhaps I would deal with them sometime later when I felt strong enough to do so, if such a time ever came. Meanwhile I would proclaim silently my will to stand firm in the faith and to rely upon whatever explanation the church itself might offer or permit in the circumstances.

"I realized that some might say that this was a cop-out, a failure to confront genuine difficulties, but on reflection I knew that this was not accurate. From reading I had done in psychology I concluded that only a radically proud individual would feel that he had all the answers at his finger tips to every possible objection to the faith. And when such difficulties were poured on, one after the other without let-up, it was ridiculous to think that they could be dealt with in a straightforward manner.

"But I soon discovered that even though I recognized my faith-illness and the subtle power of my sick pride it was not enough merely to tell myself that I was ill and therefore unable to deal adequately with the difficulties. The difficulties did not respect my illness and continued to make their presence felt regardless of my indisposition.

"It was then that I felt it necessary to 'blind' myself. I kept saying to myself that I must be blind to difficulties and not give them even a moment's glance of the mind. I accustomed myself to the notion that these challenges to faith were like a blind man's fantasies of vision which, if he followed them or even entertained them for a moment, might lead him to destruction. I cultivated a blindness which allowed me just one glimmer of light, a distant pale blue light at the end of the tunnel, a light of faith which, if I followed it, would lead me forward on a straight path until at last I might emerge into the sunlight of unquestioning belief. To allow myself to be dazzled even for a moment by false visions would, I realized, be disastrous.

"In conjunction with this I learned not to expose myself to the arrows of the enemy. By this, I mean that I eliminated all mental pronouncements about the faith, explanations to myself of why this or that belief was true, or other ruminations or reflections pertaining to matters of belief. The reason for this was obvious: the more I engaged in inner proclamations of one sort or another, the more I exposed myself to inner questions about what I had proclaimed. I learned to encapsulate my faith in one simple phrase: 'I believe according to the teachings of the church.' That was it. And I offered no reasons, no explanations, no analyses. I followed that simple light to the end and, at last, I emerged."

The example of this man reflects the simple humility of the roadside beggar: "I believe, Lord. Help Thou my unbelief."

42.

DEATH AND LIFE

Preachers and spiritual writers have long recognized that meditation on death can often be a salutary source of strength toward living a better life. At the beginning of Lent, when the church places ashes on our foreheads and reminds us that we are dust and unto dust we shall return, she is not performing some morbid rite but expressing a truth which, because it is so profound, seems very often to escape our realization. Like many profound statements it seems banal and obvious on the surface and therefore is likely to be disregarded in practice.

Our conscious minds instinctively turn away from the thought of death to concentrate on the present project. This no doubt is necessary and healthy but at least an occasional meditation on the implications of death cannot fail to heighten our consciousness of the significance of our actions and attitudes here and now. Although a morbid spirit is not to be desired, a sensitive awareness of the reality of death can well be a constructive force in more fruitful living.

Reflection on death immediately reminds us of our basic vulnerability, something to which we have already referred in a previous chapter. From the very moment of our existence until the moment of death we are always subject to injury if not to total destruction. This is the very nature of the human condition and yet surprisingly enough the injury or death in the family always seems to be a source of amazement and surprise. We de-

velop a sort of illusion of limitless continuity. Although we would
not admit it in rational discourse we instinctively assume that we
will go on in good health and good life. Thus when illness strikes
or, worse still, death, particularly in the case of someone we love,
we are stunned, filled with a sense of the unfairness of it all. When
someone very dear to us dies, we have a struggle not to blaspheme
God for His injustice in depriving this person of earthly life. Yet
we knew that anyone of us was subject to dissolution at any point.
But we have terrible difficulty in accepting this when the principle
is applied in our own circle of relatives or friends. We are like
individuals who enter into a game knowing the rules and yet
complain when the rules are applied to their apparent disad-
vantage.

Here we have the ambiguity of the whole human person: the
mind with its groping for transcendent truth, the will with its
pursuit of limitless good, the personality with its timeless identity, all cry out for continuity, for life without end. And yet we
know that our mortal bodies are subject to instant dissolution,
from a germ, a bullet in the heart or brain, or the application of
pressure on a vital organ. We hang, as it were, by a thread. The
marvel is not so much that we die but that we continue to live
so long, as a rule. And yet death seems so contrary to our essential nature as persons. Only in this context do we come to appreciate the significance of Christ's proclamation: "I am the Resurrection and the life. He that believeth in Me, though he be dead,
shall live."

There are many positive values, however, in meditating on our
vulnerability in this life. Such a reflection helps to remove the
anxiety and tension which can arise from an effort to preserve
the non-preservable, to render the vulnerable invulnerable. If we
accept the fact of our vulnerability then pain and even death lose
their power of shock, of surprise, and stimulation to rebel. The
peaceful acceptance of reality always releases positive, constructive forces that, paradoxically in this case, are life-enhancing. To
have a deep sense of one's vulnerability is to be well-adjusted to
the life situation as it really is.

A second reflection on death is related to the sense of proportion and perspective which it gives us regarding the trials and opportunities of the present moment. The person who has a deep sense of mortality will, when the situation warrants, be able to ask himself the question: "How will this situation, act, attitude, commitment, appear on my death bed?" This was known by the philosophers and theologians as seeing things "sub specie aeternitatis." An ant viewed under a microscope seems enormous. The same ant pictured against the background of a mountain may be barely visible. For some people every crisis in life seems like the end of the world. A year later many of them would be hard put to remember the circumstances and the difficulty. One wonders how many sins could have been avoided, how many suicides would not have been committed, if the individuals involved had taken the long view. There is little doubt that many people tend to minimize their moral obligations, to maximize their pleasures of the moment, to exaggerate their complaints, and to hold down their thankfulness. They tend to waste their energies and efforts, and even anxieties, in many things which have little relevance in terms of what is really lasting and valuable in life. Meditation on death can give a salutary perspective, a helpful insight into where true emphasis should be placed. One of the saddest things about dying must be the realization of how stupidly one has used the possibilities of living.

A third helpful reflection on death flows from what has already been said. This reflection stresses the brevity of living time on earth and therefore the importance of taking the best advantage of the opportunities available. From the perspective of death one sees immediately that life is amazingly short, a conviction which is heightened by an awareness of human history. Human beings are almost in the position of visitors for a brief stay on earth. Their time therefore must be budgeted intelligently. Like visitors, they must be characterized by a wondering appreciation of that which surrounds them. And since they have so little time, they must exercise considerable discrimination in what they choose to be and do and how they choose to live. Just as it would be absurd for a one-time visitor to Rome to spend his entire time in the cellar of a boarding house, so too the earthly visitor must avoid wasting his life on petty trivialities, failing to seize the grand opportunities which open out to him.

"I shall not pass this way again." An opportunity for loving service will never again be present in the same context. Life is filled with opportunities to know, to understand, to share, to communicate, to bless. The nourishing of the body of Christ, the building up of the kingdom of God, such opportunities exist on every side. But we tend to say, "tomorrow" or, "I am busy now with something else; later, later on I will do it." And the time slips by and the opportunities disappear and we find that we have indeed been in Rome but have spent most of our time in a cellar, playing foolish and meaningless games, devoting our principal efforts and energies to a sort of human ping-pong.

Reflections on death can indeed be healthful in many ways. We can look upon death as the hoped-for end of pain, the completion of the work that God has given us to do in this life, the attainment of personal fulfillment and joy, and most of all, face-to-face realization of the union with God which, we trust, we have already begun here on earth.

Meditation on death need not be morbid or depressing. Certainly death is not so when viewed in the light of Christ's teaching and promises. One would do well, when thinking of death, to keep in mind the words in the third chapter of St. John's Gospel: "God so loved the world that He sent His only-begotten Son that whosoever believes in Him may not perish, but may have everlasting life."